THE
ABC's
OF EMOTIONS

a guide to understanding how people think and feel

MARION MEYERS

DESTINY IMAGE® EUROPE
Via Maiella, 1
66020 San Giovanni Teatino (Ch) - Italy

ISBN 10: 88-89127-32-5
ISBN 13: 978-88-89127-32-2

For Worldwide Distribution. Printed in Italy.
1 2 3 4 5 6 7 8/10 09 08 07 06

This book and all other Destiny Image Europe books are available at Christian bookstores and distributors worldwide.

To order products, or for any other correspondence:

DESTINY IMAGE® EUROPE
Via Acquacorrente, 6
65123 - Pescara - Italy
Tel. +39 085 4716623 - Fax: +39 085 4716622
E-mail: info@eurodestinyimage.com

Or reach us on the Internet:

www.eurodestinyimage.com

Acknowledgements

First, to my wonderful and RGL husband—thank you for all your support and hard work; we both know I couldn't have done this without you.

And then, to some incredible ladies in my life who have modeled such competence, compassion, and courage:

- Margaret de Kort, my mom—thank you for ALL you have given me but especially for your strength. You have helped me become all I am.

- Veronica—I thank God for allowing our destinies to intertwine from time to time.

- My WIT ladies—thank you for all your invaluable help and support. Teamwork has really made this dream work. It is for you and those like you that I do all that I do.

- And finally, to my dear friend, Andrea Kelly—I know you would be so proud that this book finally made it to print. I am so much the richer for having known you. I will always love you and miss you.

Table of Contents

Foreword 7

Preface 9

Chapter 1   *Analyzing Anger* 11

Chapter 2   *Beating Bitterness* 17

Chapter 3   *Coping With Control* 25

Chapter 4   *Dealing With Depression* 31

Chapter 5   *Escaping Envy* 37

Chapter 6   *Facing Fear* 43

Chapter 7   *Governing Guilt* 49

Chapter 8   *Handling Hurt* 55

Chapter 9   *Identifying Insecurity* 61

Chapter 10   *Judgmental or Joyful* 67

Chapter 11   *Kaleidoscope of Emotions* 73

Chapter 12   *Lost in Loneliness* 81

Chapter 13   *Mourning by Morning* 89

Chapter 14   *Needy by Nature* 97

Chapter 15   *Overwhelmed or Overcoming* 103

Chapter 16   *Pitiful or Powerful* 111

Chapter 17   *Quarrelsome or Quiet* 117

Chapter 18   *Rejected or Restored* 123

Chapter 19   *Suffering Shame* 129

Chapter 20   *Tormented or Tranquil* 135

Chapter 21   *Understanding and Being Understood* 141

Chapter 22   *Vague or Visionary* 147

Chapter 23   *Worried and Weary* 153

Chapter 24   *X-hausted and Anxious* 159

Chapter 25   *Yielding Your Yesterdays* 165

Chapter 26   *Zealous for God* 171

Bibliography 173

Foreword

This A-Z multivitamin catalogue for the emotions is a book which has been long needed. The lives of many people, even Christian believers, are blighted by the devastation caused by giving vent to cynical emotional feelings and an inability to shield themselves from the enemy's attack through disconsolate melancholic depression. Small wonder that Scripture is full of admonitions—to guard our emotions, weigh our spoken words, disinfect our thoughts by dwelling only on things that enhance our living, and brighten the outlook. Emotions are powerful. They have dynamic force to either bless and enrich associations, or explode and cause infinite harm and devastation. A spoken word that cannot be withdrawn can easily break up homes, marriages, and all kinds of relationships.

This book teaches us how to control all kinds of negativism. It is an extension of our Lord's instruction and the apostle Paul's teaching on denying the flesh its free expression that causes devastation, and to be transformed by the renewing of our minds. We are responsible for all our actions and particularly every vocal and visual reaction. Our internal feelings more often than not should not see the light of day and are best left unexpressed.

I highly commend this book, written by a successful practitioner who is experienced in the world of social services and the church, and has widely dealt with both churched and unchurched people. Reading one chapter each day will provide a safety net for guaranteed emotional health for both young and old.

Rev. Wynne Lewis
1980 - 1991 Senior Minister, Kensington Temple, London
1991 - 2000 General Superintendent Elim Pentecostal Churches, UK

Preface

We live in a time of technological revolution. The growth or increase of knowledge and information is of astronomical proportions compared to any other time in our human history. At the very same time, however, I believe we are experiencing a complete meltdown of relationships and family values. I say this not so we can look on in pious indignation, pronounce judgment, or declare in self-righteousness that the moral decline of our society is terrible, but rather so we can sound the alarm and be involved in the solution. Insecurity and brokenness in people's lives are of epidemic proportions, caused by marital breakdowns, teenage pregnancies and abortion, abuse of all forms, loneliness and isolation, self-harm, and suicide, just to mention a few.

Because churches should be a hospital for the hurting, broken, and sick, there would seem to be proportionally more damaged and dysfunctional people in church than in the world. I believe our God welcomes all these from the highways and byways of life to come into His house and feast on His healing power and goodness. Once these people are healed and strengthened in the Lord, I believe He wants these same people to minister to others around them. It is problematic, however, when many in the Body of Christ are so caught up in their own brokenness and dysfunction that they are unable to look beyond themselves and their problems. Consequently, it is my heart's desire to bring counsel to them from the Word of God—still the best handbook on human behavior. God can bring healing to every area of our damaged souls. And when God arms us with His wisdom, insight, and truth, then we can further be equipped, empowered, and released into our God-given destinies so that we can turn this world the right way up for our precious Lord.

While co-pastoring a church with my husband and raising two wonderful teenagers, both of whom have taken up a considerable amount of my time, I have also taken four years to write this book. Drawing from my passion for helping people and the wealth of experience gained over the past 21 years as a social worker and a full-time minister. In this book, I have used the alphabet to cover a wide range of emotional topics and issues. It is by no means exhaustive in its scope, nor could any book be.

This book is written in such a way that you can read all 26 chapters in subsequent order, or you can select one or more chapters that you feel a special pull toward. In any case, it is my prayer that every chapter will touch your life in some way and make you more whole. Whether you are facing issues in your life or equipping yourself to minister more effectively to those around you who are struggling with certain issues, I am sure this book will help you because it has already set so many free. Remember that whatever God does in you He wants to do through you too. He saves you so that you can minister salvation to others; He heals you so that you can pray for others; He ministers His peace, joy, and freedom to your heart so that you can minister the same to those around you. Be encouraged because God is just waiting to turn your misery into your ministry and your pain into your passion.

> *But I have prayed especially for you...that your {own} faith may not fail; and when you yourself have turned again, strengthen and establish your brethren* (Luke 22:32).

Marion Meyers
Exeter, United Kingdom

Chapter 1

ANALYZING ANGER

ANGER IS DEFINED AS A "STRONG FEELING CAUSED BY AN INJURY," literally meaning, "the strongest of all passions." Anger can be our friend, indicating to us when something is wrong. Indeed, if we didn't have this emotion, we wouldn't react when we were being wronged. Additionally, it can motivate us to become more assertive in our relationships and help us change bad habits or situations.

Anger can also be an enemy. Because its manifestations can range from mild irritation to rage and violence, we need to understand the destructive power of this emotion and master it. A person under the influence of anger can cause great hurt and hardship to himself and others. Matthew Henry says, *"An angry man stirs up strife, is troublesome and quarrelsome in the family and in the neighbourhood, blows the coals, and even forces those to fall out with him that would live peaceable and quietly by him"* (Prov. 29:22; 27:4 Matthew Henry's Commentary).

Many of us, when we were children, learned ineffective coping skills from poor role models, and now as adults, we are consequently inadequate and un-skilled in dealing with the often destructive emotion of anger. Many parents don't allow the healthy expression of anger in their children, labeling them "cheeky" or "rebellious" because the portrayal of anger is considered as too strong, negative, threatening, or unacceptable an emotion. Dr. Henry Brandt, one of the leading psychologists in the United States, suggests anger is in-volved in 80 to 90 percent of all counselling problems. It is interesting to note that it is possible to be angry and not depressed, but impossible to be depressed and not angry.

Many studies have proven that anger and hostility over a long-term period can be deadly and may bring on psychosomatic illnesses and aggravate life-threatening diseases.[1] The Bible confirms this: *"A calm and undisturbed mind and heart are the life and health of the body, but envy, jealousy, and wrath are like rottenness of the bones"* (Prov. 14:30). While it isn't possible or healthy to totally get rid of anger, we can learn how to master it. Fortunately, God's instruction manual (the Bible) gives us understanding into this powerful emotion.

WHAT CAN WE DO?

We cannot change the past, the people around us, or what happens to us, but we can change what happens *in us.*

- ⌐ Processing the past will stop anger from being your constant companion.

- ⌐ Self-insight will bring you understanding and deliverance.

- ⌐ Learning more effective behavioral skills will help to bridle your tongue and master this emotion.

- ⌐ Using anger as a friend will help you to gain control over it rather than dealing with an enemy who controls you.

"He who has no rule over his own spirit is like a city that is broken down and without walls" (Prov. 25:28). Matthew Henry adds to the seriousness of this Scripture: *"All that is good goes out, and forsakes him; all that is evil breaks in upon him. He lies exposed to all the temptations of Satan and becomes an easy prey to that enemy;"* (Prov. 25:28 Matthew Henry's Commentary).

ROOT CAUSES OF ANGER

Up to 75 percent of expressed anger is due to past hurts, while only 25 percent is due to our current situation. Consequently, we realize that many times we force our present relationships to pay us a debt that they don't owe.[2] Take heed—fretting over yesterday will produce only a harvest of evil in our lives (see Ps. 37:8).

Part of our problem is we feel justified in our anger, as though we have a right to be angry and blame others for our difficulties. Yet these thoughts and attitudes only serve to add more fuel to our anger. Life *is* unfair, unjust, and harsh to many people. In fact, you don't have to be a "bad" person to have "bad" things happen to you; you just have to be a person!

Paul said to the Ephesians, *"If you are angry do not sin by nursing your grudge, get over it quickly otherwise you will give the devil a mighty foothold"* (Eph. 4:26-27, author's paraphrase; see also TLB and AMP). Do most of us listen to this advice? Or do we rather make things worse because we nurture our grudge and give the devil a foothold in our lives, which soon becomes a stronghold? On the other hand, letting go of an offense quickly is the least harmful way for us to handle any hurt we may experience.

While *past and present causes* for our anger include external events and people, it's those internal issues that cause us the most harm—like being angry at ourselves for our stupid mistakes, failures, and weaknesses. Another example is getting angry, which results from jealousy or envy, because we compete and compare ourselves with others and come up short. Self-hatred and self-rejection produce a rotten harvest of anger in our lives. However, the root cause of anger is the sin nature that centers on self—"I want *what* I want, *when* I want it, and *how* I want it." If this is your thinking pattern, you are setting yourself up to be a "victim of unfairness," which will constantly produce anger in you.

IS ANGER SINFUL?

Nowhere in the Bible does it state that anger in itself is sinful. God became angry at the Israelites' disobedience and sin, and Jesus was angry at the hard-heartedness of the religious sect. The apostle Paul does not forbid anger, but says *"when"* you are angry, do not sin. It is our reaction when we are angry that causes us to sin.

UNGODLY REACTIONS TO ANGER

Exploders

When people "explode," their anger is uncontrolled and unrestrained. It is cruel and overwhelming and very harsh toward those on the receiving end. Exploders are at the mercy of their own temper and have no rule over their own spirit (see Prov. 25:28). Scripture refers to this type of person as a fool (see Prov. 14:17,29; 29:11).

Exploders often try to justify and excuse their behavior, but psychologists agree that it is not beneficial to "let rip," as this only escalates the problem and doesn't resolve the situation. Epictetus wrote, "Whenever you are angry, be assured that it is not only a present evil, but you have increased the habit."[3] When exploders throw a temper tantrum, it is similar to a toddler throwing all his toys out of a box. When they insist that they "cannot help it," they believe and act like victims of their own tempers, but God is well able to help anyone be an overcomer in this area of life if they are willing.

Suppressors

These people seethe inwardly; they clam up, cave in, implode, or suppress their anger. Although the exploders are more threatening, suppressors who have buried their emotions deep are extremely difficult to reach. They often exist in a denial mode and refuse to admit they are angry. Suppressors mask their anger in different nonverbal ways, such as sulking, putting emotional walls up, watching inordinate amounts of television, hiding in literature, or using body language such as rolled eyes, gritted teeth, or rude hand signals. Instead of displaying their anger in more spectacular ways, they can be grumpy, irritable, sarcastic, and critical. In any case, if you are retaining anger, you have nothing to give away in your relationships *except* anger.

Many can alternate from being a suppressor to an exploder, at one time suppressing everything and then aggressively exploding at another time, at which point they have little control, This anger is often out of proportion to the offense and often over the innocent. They may blame someone or something else for their bad behavior and refuse to take any responsibility for themselves. They see themselves as victims of circumstances and people and will not change.

SOLUTIONS

Confession

Confession and repentance of sin are the first steps toward breakthrough in this area of your life (see James 5:16; 1 John 1:9). But no one can help you if you remain in denial. You need to acknowledge and "own" your anger, no longer resorting to excuses or playing blame-games. Only the truth can set you free (see John 8:32). Confess your angry reactions and behavior as sin. They are works of the flesh that are opposed and antagonistic toward God and do not promote the righteousness He requires (see Gal. 5:19-21; James 1:20).

Ask God for His Help

James says, *"You do not have because you do not ask"* (James 4:2 NKJV). When we ask, He will give us the grace to overcome not only in stress-free circumstances but also in adversity and trials. We do have the ability with His power, to stay calm in adversity (see Acts 1:8; Ps. 94:13); and we can *"endure whatever comes {whatever trials and temptations}, with good temper"* (Col. 3:12b).

Losing control and using anger to emotionally abuse others are never justifiable. As the victim of an angry person, don't allow the offender to excuse their anger as being your fault. Their blaming you and your acceptance of the blame perpetuate the problem and prevent them from taking responsibility, thereby keeping both parties victims.

Forgive Your Offenders and Overlook the Offense

We now need to forgive or "let it drop." Many people remain angry about things that happened many years ago or at people who may have already died. The victim of your anger may not even know that you are angry with them, or if they do know, they may not care. Don't allow these people to continue to hold you ransom to the hurt they have caused you.

Jesus said forgive "seventy times seven" (see Matt. 18:22). In our language, that means frequently, often, or over and over. The only thing not allowing you to forgive is your pride (see Prov. 13:10). The Bible clearly instructs on this matter: *"Above all things have intense and unfailing love for one another, for love covers a multitude of sins {forgives and disregards the offenses of others}"* (1 Pet. 4:8). Remember, we are not passively suppressing or forgetting the offense, but we are actively choosing to forgive and overlook it.

Listen, then Speak

It is not a coincidence that God has given us two ears and one mouth. Because anger quickly becomes irrational and causes us to jump to conclusions, we must be doers of His Word and be quick to listen and slow to speak. In this way, we will learn the vital skill of becoming slow to anger (see James 1:19). Besides this, the Bible tells us that it is a fool who is quick to speak and answers a matter before he has heard it (see Prov. 18:13). The apostle Paul warns us, *"When you are angry don't sin. Don't let the sun go down on your anger"* (see Eph. 4:26-27 TLB and AMP). He knew that it would be easy to sin when we get angry and that we would need to get over it as quickly as possible so that it would not lead us into trouble.

You are considered to be a wise person with great understanding when you "still" and "restrain" your anger (see Prov. 14:29; 19:11; 29:11). First, thoroughly consider all the merits and extenuating circumstances before coming to a conclusion. Wisdom says to slow down and think your response through. Listen to what is being said—verbally and nonverbally—before responding.

Keeping things in context with well-balanced logic and a temperate attitude will always defeat irrational anger and stop you from being devoured by your enemy, the devil (see 2 Tim. 1:7; 1 Pet. 5:8). The whole world is not out to get you, and no, all the traffic has not conspired to frustrate you!

Although we must be slow to speak, we must also be assertive and confront when necessary. Responding with a "soft" answer will be far more effective than harsh words that just serve to stir up anger (see Prov. 15:1). Remember, *it is the passion and temper of anger that is the problem and causes us to sin, not anger itself.* We can, as the Bible says, speak the truth in love and put away lying (falsity), speaking truth with our neighbor (see Eph. 4:15,25). Your driving motivation must be to resolve the conflict and gain understanding and not to punish the person. We must pursue peace and restoration, not revenge or retaliation (see 1 Pet. 3:11; Rom. 12:19).

This poem, by William Blake, has helped me to be assertive:

> I was angry with my friend,
> I told my wrath, my wrath did end;
> I was angry with my foe,
> I told it not, my wrath did grow.

Do not allow your fear of man, fear of rejection, or fear of failure make you passive. The anger resulting from the offense is toxic and will hurt you far more than not being assertive. You can choose your reaction—implode and/or explode, or do it God's way.

ENDNOTES

1. Dr. S.I. McMillen, *None of These Diseases* (Westwood, NJ: Spire Books, 1963), 205-210 paraphrased.

2. Bob Phillips, *Controlling Your Emotions Before They Control You*, (Eugene, OR: Harvest House Publishers, 1995), 88 paraphrased.

3. Epictetus, *a Roman (Greek-born) slave & Stoic philosopher (55 AD - 135 AD)*: http://www.quotationspage.com/quotes/Epictetus/

Chapter 2

BEATING BITTERNESS

"No matter what you've experienced,
remember this: there are people who've had it
better than you and done worse. And there are people
who've had it worse and done better. Past hurts can
make you bitter or better—the choice is always yours!"[1]

RECOGNIZING BITTERNESS

IN THE BOOK OF EXODUS, *BITTERNESS* IS DEFINED as something that is "opposed to sweetness" (see Exod. 15:23); in Proverbs, it means "a deep sorrow
and heaviness of spirit" (see Prov. 14:10); in Samuel, it is "a thing that produces dreadful effects" (see 2 Sam. 2:26); and in Acts, it speaks about the "gall
of bitterness," which is "a state that is most offensive and distasteful to God"
(see Acts 8:23).

The bitterness we are dealing with is "a violent inward displeasure against
another."[2] The Bible instructs us to: *"Let all bitterness and...wrath (passion,
rage, bad temper) and resentment...and slander (evil-speaking...) be banished from
you, with all malice (spite, ill will)..."* (Eph. 4:31).

Bitterness can never be a friend or helpful to us, as anger can. It is our
enemy and one of the unhealthiest emotions we can possess. Bitterness is emotional suicide. It troubles our minds with memories and tortures like splinters

twisting in our minds. Bitterness can also be likened to the act of drinking poison while hoping the other person will die.

Bitterness is an offense that is harbored until it develops roots and holds onto you. Jeremiah warns us that our evil thoughts will get stuck to the point that we will be unable to dislodge them (see Jer. 4:14). Being progressive in nature, bitterness can start as a small feeling, but left unchecked, it will consume our thoughts, tormenting and harassing us until it controls our entire attitude toward life and people.

How do you recognize bitterness? Like David, ask God to: *"Search me {thoroughly} O God, and know my heart!"* (Ps. 139:23a). Ask yourself if there is someone you literally cannot stand to be around. Is there someone you avoid at all costs? Is there someone you can't find any good in? Is there someone you think evil thoughts of and constantly speak evil of?

Our words reveal bitterness within ourselves: *"Their mouth is full of cursing and bitterness"* (Rom. 3:14). Are you unkind, sarcastic, and angry at others or God? Do you have constant thoughts of getting even and taking revenge? If so, these thoughts will eventually turn into actions. *"For out of the abundance of the heart the mouth speaks. A good man out of the good treasure of his heart brings forth good things, and an evil man out of the evil treasure brings forth evil things"* (Matt. 12:34b-35 NKJV).

THE ROOTS OF BITTERNESS

Hurtful Words

Hurting people hurt people by the words they speak. *"There are those who speak rashly, like the piercing of a sword"* (Prov. 12:18a); and *"grievous words stir up anger"* (Prov. 15:1b). Insensitive, unkind, unloving, abusive, sarcastic words injure and pierce us like a sword, especially from those we love, trust, and have close relationship with. Words can make us feel unworthy and of no value, which causes emotional harm.

Hurtful Actions

Just as hurtful words, unintended or deliberate, can damage us, so can hurtful actions, whether perceived or actual. Job's story is a good example of "perceived but not actual" hurtful actions. Job thought God was destroying him and so he became embittered toward God.

When we face trauma or loss in our lives, we could, like Job, blame God and become bitter toward Him. Do you feel that God should have done something to stop the abuse, the hurt, or the tragedy? Where was He when you needed Him? Questions like these will embitter you toward God. God doesn't always give us the answers to our questions, but we can be sure that He is a good God and He wants only what is good for us. Accusing God unjustly will only compound our problems as it disconnects us from the One who is there to help and strengthen us in our time of need.

Maybe you feel like Cain who thought God had dealt unfairly with him, and consequently, he became jealous of his brother. He harbored resentment, carefully nurturing and watering it with thoughts of revenge until finally his plant of bitterness and hatred produced the fruit of premeditated murder (see Gen. 4:8).

THE RESULTS OF BITTERNESS

Bitterness Makes Us Foolish

At times, our bitterness may feel pleasurable because the devil can deceive us into thinking that we have a right to our indignation and self-pity. But bitterness is unreasonable; it will make you do and say stupid things. It is foolish to harbor a grudge (see Eccl. 7:9). Bitterness will never change the past, never correct the problem, and never restore your loss or heal your pain; it will only make it worse.

Bitterness Hurts Our Relationships

"Pursue peace with all people, and holiness, without which no one will see the Lord: looking carefully lest anyone fall short of the grace of God; **lest any root of bitterness springing up cause trouble, and by this many become defiled"** (Heb. 12:14-15 NKJV, emphasis added). Bitterness is exceptionally harmful to our relationships, and negatively affects our overall attitude, sense of happiness and joy. When people get divorced, it generally boils down to bitterness. In the Bible, couples are warned, *"not* [to] *be harsh or bitter or resentful toward {each other}"* (Col. 3:19b).

Bitterness is the inevitable consequence of not processing hurts in our relationships. These unprocessed hurts, compounded by unresolved issues and nurtured by worrying, will lead to the breakdown of any relationship. It is very important to resist the devil at his onset (see James 4:7), and deal with bitterness before it takes root in your life.

Bitterness Makes Us Miserable

"Their mouth is full of cursing and bitterness. Their feet are swift to shed blood. Destruction...and misery mark their ways" (Rom. 3:14-16). Bitterness will affect

you, whether you are awake or asleep (see Isa. 38:15). Physically, bitterness will cause you to struggle with fatigue, backache, ulcers, headaches, and many other related illnesses and drain you of vitality and energy (see Prov. 14:30). We begin to die inside when we harbor resentment and bitterness and hold onto thoughts of revenge.

> The moment I start hating a man I become his slave. I can't enjoy my work anymore because he even controls my thoughts. My resentments produce too many stress hormones in my body and I am fatigued after only a few hours of work. The work I formerly enjoyed is now drudgery. Even vacations cease to bring me pleasure. It may be a luxurious car that I drive along a scenic route but as far as my experience of pleasure is concerned, I might as well be driving a wagon in mud and rain. The man I hate hounds me wherever I go. I can't escape his tyrannical grasp on my mind. When the waiter serves me steak and fries and salad with strawberries and ice-cream, it might as well be stale bread and water. My teeth chew the food and I swallow it, but the man I hate will not permit me to enjoy it. The man I hate may be miles away from my bedroom, but crueler than any slave driver, he whips my thoughts into such a frenzy that my innerspring mattress becomes a rack of torture. The lowliest of the serfs can sleep but not I. I really must acknowledge the fact that I am a slave to every man on whom I pour the vials of my wrath.[3]

Bitterness Will Destroy Your Relationship With God and Steal Your Salvation

God is a God of hearts. God doesn't live and fellowship with you in your head; He lives in your heart, He talks to you in your heart, He loves you and strengthens you in your heart. However, when your heart is filled with bitterness, then God cannot fellowship with you. He cannot lead or guide you, as your need for revenge and repaying evil for evil is what consumes and directs you.

We are to love, serve, trust, and believe Him with *all* our hearts. The devil would deceive us into tolerating our bitterness, but we must fight it. We must fight unforgiveness because it will destroy our relationship with God. And when we finally get rid of our bitterness, we will be amazed how we grow in our relationship with God.

RESOLVING BITTERNESS

Acknowledge that you have become or you are becoming bitter. You have to first face it and own it before any healing can take place. M. Scott Peck wrote, "This tendency to avoid problems and the emotional suffering inherent in them is the primary basis of all mental illness."[4] Bob Phillips in his book, *Controlling Your Emotions Before They Control You*, elaborates on this thought: "Mental and emotional, and spiritual growth come from facing problems rather than running from them. It involves struggle, pain, and courage. It requires exercise of the will and the determination to not give up. Out of the battles and conflicts of life our spirit and character are molded. When we accept responsibility for our own actions and attitudes, we grow toward maturity. We gain self-respect and begin to adjust to the pain that is common to all people."[5]

Confess and Repent

Job's deliverance started when he confessed to God: "Listen to my bitter complaint; don't condemn me God" (see Job 10:1-2). We often internalize and repress our feelings when instead we should be confessing and communicating them. Honest confession and sincere repentance take courage and determination, and bring you the healing you have been longing for.

Grant Forgiveness

This is not a feeling, but a promise or commitment.

Have you ever heard people say, "You haven't truly forgiven an offense if you haven't forgotten it"? This is not necessarily true as forgiveness does not depend on our forgetting it. It is true to say that we will sometimes never forget! David Augsburger says: "Forgiveness is not holy amnesia which erases the past, instead it is the experience of healing that draws the poison out; you may recall the hurt but you will not relive the pain. The hornet of memory may fly again but forgiveness has drawn out the sting."[6]

Forgiving yourself is also just as important. If the Greater One can forgive you, then you can forgive yourself. Respect the blood of Jesus for what it is—powerful and able to wash you as white as snow, no matter what the sin.

Understanding the Purpose of God

Understanding the purpose of God will set you free from bitterness. Joseph knew the purposes of God amidst his trials, betrayal, and hardships and did not allow bitterness, which could have been personally justified, to take hold of his heart. He could have been consumed with bitterness, but when he was reunited with his brothers, who had first betrayed him, he held no bitterness toward them. *"But now, do not therefore be grieved or angry with yourselves because you sold me here; for God sent me before you to preserve life. ...So now it was not you who sent me here, but God"* (Gen. 45:5,8a NKJV).

The apostle Paul could have easily been consumed with bitterness toward those who mistreated him, but in humiliating circumstances in prison he wrote:

> *I have been through so many difficult times that I could easily have become bitter; however, through it all, I understood the purpose and plan of God. Indeed we have the sentence of death in ourselves but that was to keep us from trusting in and depending on ourselves instead of on God who raises the dead* (2 Cor. 1:8-9 author's paraphrase).

We too should be able to say, *"And we know that all things work together for good to those...who are the called according to His purpose"* (Rom. 8:28 NKJV).

Following is a modern-day Joseph story.

> The worst part of the woman's pregnancy was the violence. A sailor raped her. Both her doctor and her attorney advised her to have an abortion. It seemed logical that an unmarried woman who had been raped should terminate the pregnancy. She believed, however, that God creates all life for a purpose. She believed even though that particular life was forced on her, it was for a special reason. She believed it would be wrong to end that life. The man who raped her was a total stranger. He did it in a drunken stupor. When the Navy found out, the sailor was instantly shipped out to sea. While she was seeking legal assistance, the rapist's wife confronted her. "If you sue him," she said, "you'll ruin my life." The woman explained, "My husband is the father of our severely retarded child. If you sue him, he'll divorce me, and I cannot care for the child alone." She did not sue. A doctor and his wife planned to adopt the baby. During the waiting time they showed Christian kindness to the young nurse. They were all three shaken when the baby was born deformed and dead. The wife and the nurse cried in each others' arms. "How close I was" the nurse said, "to becoming utterly consumed with bitterness." Human logic would say she would stay away from babies for the rest of her life. Human logic would be wrong. She works in a hospital delivery room and through her tragedy, she now helps parents of stillborn and badly deformed babies. She reassures

those grieving parents, "Don't let this make you bitter. God will use it to bless you. He blessed me."[7]

ENDNOTES

1. John Maxwell, *Failing Forwards* (Nashville, TN: Nelson Publishers, 2000), 80-81.

2. Matthew Henry, *Henry's Commentary on the Whole Bible: New Modern Edition*, (Electronic Database. Copyright © 1991 by Hendrickson Publishers, Inc.).

3. S.I. McMillen, *None of These Diseases* (Westwood, NJ: Spire Books, 1963), 73-74.

4. M. Scott Peck, *The Road Less Travelled:25th Anniversary Edition, A new Psychology of Love, Traditional Values and Spiritual Growth*, (New York, NY: Touchstone Books 1978), 16-17.

5. Bob Phillips, *Controlling Your Emotions Before They Control You* (Eugene, OR: Harvest House Publishers, 1995), 31.

6. David Augsburger, *The Freedom of Forgiveness,* (Chicago, IL: Moody Publishers, 1988).

7. David Sisler, *Overcoming Bitterness* http://davidsisler.com/08-06-2001.htm

Chapter 3

COPING WITH CONTROL

CONTROL CHECKLIST

❏ Are you feeling frustrated, restricted, crushed, or deflated?

❏ Do someone else's expectations of you weigh you down?

❏ Is that person's obsessiveness and possessiveness of you exhausting?

❏ Are you constantly jealous and envious of a friend when he or she spends time with someone else?

❏ Do you often have temper tantrums?

❏ Do you feel smothered? Or do you hold on too tightly to someone and feel very dependent on them?

❏ Do you often feel intimidated by someone close to you? Is that person constantly harsh to you and use bad language?

❏ Do you often threaten or sulk and withhold affection and intimacy?

❏ Are you fearful of upsetting the mood in the house or the mood of your spouse?

❏ Is there someone always interfering in your life, and are the boundaries confused? Have you been told you are interfering?

❏ Have you been told you are critical, opinionated, and/or often complaining?

❏ Do you find it difficult to trust God to intervene and feel more dependent on others than God?

❏ Do you always have an uncontrollable urge to take over or lead?

If you said yes to more than a couple of these questions, then this chapter will offer you truth that will set you free from control.

God hates control and manipulation because it is the mode of operation the devil uses to force his will on others. Domination, manipulation, and unscriptural control cause destructive and unhealthy relationships. When we succumb to *control* through the fear of man and choose man's approval rather than God's, we are practicing a form of idolatry. When we act as the *controller*, and attempt to exert our power beyond what God has ordered or ordained, we are rebellious. The Bible calls both of these instances "witchcraft" (see 1 Sam. 15:23).

Insecure people are likely to control, or be controlled, or do both. And with insecurity reaching epidemic proportions today, control and manipulation are rampant. It is time we regained our freedom. *"1 Stand fast therefore in the liberty by which Christ has made us free, and do not be entangled again with a yoke of bondage".* (Gal. 5:1 NKJV).

COMPREHENDING CONTROL

People exercise varying amounts of power or authority over others depending on the situation. In Genesis, God made humans to be kings and rulers over all the works of His hand (see Gen. 1:26); and the psalmist says that God has placed all things under our feet (see Ps. 8:6). The only time control of people is acceptable is when God has ordered it. Whereas seeking a power or attempting to extend a sphere of dominion over and against what God originally intended is rebellion against the boundaries set by God. Rightful authority would be a loving parent imposing discipline on a disobedient child. The correction from a spiritual leader is another example as it ensures the will of God is fulfilled in our lives. The enemy, however, will use every opportunity to bring imbalance and abuse into our relationships so that he can destroy them.

In Webster's Dictionary, the word *control* means "to direct, influence and exercise authority over or to restrain, keep within bounds, regulations." *Manipulation* defined is "to manage or influence shrewdly or divisively, to control or tamper with by skilled use for personal gain."

The serpent shrewdly manipulated Eve into questioning God's control and rule over her life. As sin came through one man to us all, it left us with a legacy that is called the sin nature (see Rom. 5:12). The ruler of this world works through the sinful nature to control the lives of many, thus making them his slaves.

ROOT CAUSES

Childhood Hurt

Childhood hurt is a contributing factor in developing ungodly patterns of behavior in our lives. Abused children become determined to not allow others to hurt them because of someone else's abuse. They either consciously or subconsciously set the rules so that they will not be hurt again.

In other cases, the emotional pain of rejection and hurt during childhood becomes so great that they will do almost anything to maintain people's approval. They, therefore, succumb knowingly to the control and manipulation while experiencing all the resentment, frustration, and bitterness that it produces.

Poor Role Models

If control and manipulation were a way of life in your parents' relationships, they have most likely become ingrained in your personality. If you respected controlling people or you were forced to take control very early in life, you have probably learned control as a natural way of relating to people.

If your role models used control, or the handing over of personal responsibility to others as a coping mechanism, you may have learned to do the same thing as an adult. God does not have a problem with us having a balanced reliance on some trustworthy people in our lives, but when it takes priority over our trust in Him, then it is unacceptable.

Boys who are "over-mothered" grow up never learning to take proper responsibility for their lives. As men, they still want their wife to mother them so they can continue to shirk their responsibilities. Mothers are particularly guilty of smothering their sons who later face dire consequences.

Selfish Ambition

Growing up with feelings of inadequacy, helplessness, and powerlessness can often cause people to develop a warped sense of power. They develop a need to always lead and be in control. This need for recognition and status will produce selfish ambition.

Cain's longing to be accepted by God caused him to manipulate and control his circumstance to the place where he murdered his brother in order to become the sole object of God's affection and approval (see Gen. 4:7). Today, we do the same by bad-mouthing and criticizing others. Although we may not physically kill anyone, we are not unlike Cain when we slander another believer's character. When you find a critical, opinionated, judgmental person, he or she is likely to be controlling and manipulative.

People who do not have their security in Christ look to other things and people to make them feel important. But take note, if you work hard to maneuver and manipulate yourself into a position, a friendship, or general popularity, you will have to work even harder to stay there.

Fear of Failure and a Lack of Faith

Fear of failure and a lack of faith will cause you to work out your problems in your own power and strength. If you do not see the solution with the eyes of faith based on the promises in God's Word, then you will attempt to force and manipulate the issue. And when you attempt to force some things in your own might and power for your own benefit, you may be trying to change some things that God never intended you to change.

THE CHARACTERISTICS OF CONTROL

Controlling With Strong Emotions

Strong language, shouting, jealousy, rage, anger, and aggressive intimidation are commonly known as the "strong emotions." The controller can also maintain his or her grip of intimidation by threatening to do something humiliating or harmful if not obeyed.

The victims accept the repression without much resistance as they fear the strong reactions. Often, compliance, submission, and obedience are secured after an initial show of force only once, and then they are maintained by the mere threat of repeated aggression or violence.

Controlling With Weak Emotions

This type of control includes tears, hurt feelings, sulking, silence, and withdrawal. It is usually the passive manipulator who will use all these tactics to play the underdog, the victim, the needy or helpless one. This person will do these things in order to manipulate others into giving them whatever they want. This may include money, time, attention, pity, or help, even if it's all at your expense. The guilt is what they play on and use to their advantage—"If you love me, you'll do this for me"; or "You don't know what I've been through"; or "You don't love me enough." Our giving into them, therefore, is not out of our generosity and love for them, but rather out of guilt. As the Bible says, we are giving reluctantly, sorrowfully and under compulsion (see 2 Cor. 9:7).

Other Forms of Manipulation

Other forms of manipulation include faking sickness, migraines, etc. Bribery is also used, especially between parents and children, and usually goes something like this: "I'll give you this if you do that...."

Flattery can be regarded as a form of manipulation as the motives behind it are often wrong. Asking yourself some honest questions such as, "What are their motives behind all this flattery, and what are they buttering me up for?" are important. A flatterer usually wants something but is not direct or straightforward about it. Rather, this person attempts to get what he or she wants in a cowardly or shrewd manner.

Controlling Through Expectations

The weight of certain expectations from others can cause us to do some things and be someone that we don't want to do or be. In the Gospels, Jesus rebuked Peter for trying to control His destiny. Although Peter was well-meaning, his expectations as a Jew caused him to reject the idea of a crucified Messiah (see Matt. 16:22). Jesus was then very direct with him and openly rebuked him for his selfish and evil motives.

Control Will Always Have Consequences

Control and manipulation happen mostly in our close relationships. The devil rarely uses people we do not care about to influence us. Remember this: When God wants to bless us, He puts a person in our lives; when the devil wants to destroy us, he puts a person in our lives.

THE CURE

In Spirit

If you have been practicing any form of witchcraft, rebellion, or idolatry, you need to confess your sins to God and repent of them. He is willing to forgive us and cleanse us of all unrighteousness (see 1 John 1:9). Secondly, if you have been the victim of control and manipulation, you will need to forgive those who have offended you in this manner. Do not let the enemy have an advantage over you because of unforgiveness and bitterness in your heart (see 2 Cor. 2:11).

Taking authority in the name of Jesus is important, as the devil is at work wherever there is ungodly control and manipulation. *"For we do not wrestle against flesh and blood, but against principalities, against powers..."* (Eph. 6:12 NKJV). We must become bold like Jesus who resisted the intimidating threats of the devil regardless of the circumstances. *"For God has not given us a spirit of fear, but of power and of love and of a sound mind"* (2 Tim. 1:7 NKJV).

Selfish ambition is offensive to God, but He can help us banish this from our hearts in prayer (James 3:14). Learning to trust God in every circumstance, problem, or storm in our lives is vital to overcoming past habits. It helps us to overcome our doubt and unbelief and stops us from trying to do everything in our own strength. If we have faith, we will know that God works out everything for our good in His time.

In Deed

Confrontation of the controller/manipulator is necessary, for without it, most people will carry on just the way they have been. However, the mere thought of confrontation may be very daunting. The minute you take back some of your freedom and set new boundaries, people will react. Patterns can be deeply ingrained; consequently, most will resist you, but be determined to push through. God constantly exhorts us in the Word not to fear but to trust Him in all circumstances. Be aware of your enemy—fear, as it will cause you to give up even before you've joined the battle (see 2 Chron. 20:17).

In wisdom, set new boundaries in your family relationships and friendships that hold you back, but do not do it alone. Find a friend who can help, support, and pray with you, and to whom you can be accountable. Friendships that cannot be restored to a healthy balance will need to be cut off; otherwise, before you know it, you will return to the old patterns of control and manipulation. We relate to people in predetermined patterns; so, without confrontation, acknowledgment, repentance, and change, these ungodly patterns will inevitably continue. However, family relationships are different, and you cannot always cut yourself off. For instance, you may live with them; thus, a supportive friend or group is essential to be able to work through the changes.

Chapter 4

DEALING WITH DEPRESSION

IF YOU HAVE NOT THOUGHT ABOUT THIS BEFORE, it is interesting to note that all the major downers start with "D" such as: diet, debt, death, disease, drugs, divorce, doubt, and destruction. Even the words *devil* and *demons* start with a "D." In addition, most of the characteristics of depression start with a "D" such as, disappointed, despondent, discouraged, disillusioned, dread, despair, and death!

Many famous people have had bouts of depression. Winston Churchill struggled with it; the great preacher, Charles Spurgeon battled it for years; and this is what Abraham Lincoln wrote: "I am now the most miserable man living. If what I feel were equally distributed to the whole human family, there would not be a cheerful face on the earth. Whether I shall ever be better, I cannot tell; I awfully forebode I shall not. To remain as I am is impossible. I must die or be better, it appears to me."[1]

We will never stop experiencing stress, concerns, difficulties, or troubles; but we can stop allowing them to control, destroy, and depress us. We must also stop using ineffective and destructive skills to deal with and overcome them. Paul had many troubles, but he didn't allow them to overcome him. *"We are hard-pressed on every side, yet not crushed; we are perplexed, but not in despair; persecuted, but not forsaken; struck down, but not destroyed"* (2 Cor. 4:8-9 NKJV).

The best biblical example illustrating depression is Elijah. At the peak of his depression, he comes to the point of ultimate despair and says, *"Now, O*

Lord, take away my life; for I am no better than my fathers" (1 Kings 19:4b). He tells God that he is giving up and that he doesn't care. His despair is not just the result of one conflict but the result of a lengthy build-up of pressures over a long period. For Elijah, it was just the "final straw."

He had come to the end of his tether, which didn't happen in a day. He was emotionally, physically, and spiritually exhausted. *"...I have been very zealous for the LORD God of hosts;* [great emotional and physical energy] *for the children of Israel have forsaken Your covenant, torn down Your altars, and killed Your prophets with the sword* [great anger and frustration]. *I alone am left* [loneliness and loss]; *and they seek to take my life* [self-pity]" (1 Kings 19:10 NKJV).

WHAT IS DEPRESSION?

The Bible doesn't use the exact word "depression," but uses similar words like "downcast," "spirit of heaviness," "a heavy, failing, and burdened spirit." David said, *"Therefore my spirit is overwhelmed within me; My heart within me is distressed"* (Ps. 143:4 NKJV); and a little later, he described his depression as *"those who go down into the pit"* (Ps. 143:7b).

Depression has been described as the "common cold" of mental health. All of us at some time or another and in varying degrees have experienced or will experience it. Bob Phillips describes it as "more than a bad day; it is the state of unhappiness; it carries with it a sense of hopelessness, and there seems to be no way out of the difficulties you face."[2]

This dismay gives rise to a loss of perspective, whereby you don't see things for what they are, as your emotions cannot be trusted. Apathy (not caring), withdrawal from people and life, oversensitivity, and misinterpreting the motivation of others, are all a part of this host of emotions called depression.

Phillips continues, "It is not a disorder of the brain or a disease but it is the result of how you view life and your life specifically. More importantly, it is a way of thinking and behaving."[3] This is good news as it means you are not a helpless victim of circumstances, but rather someone who can be in charge of his own emotions and destiny and one who is able to make the necessary changes. Depression may come from hurt, loss, anger, or guilt that has been turned inward and not properly dealt with.

Webster's definition of *depress* is "to lower, to sadden, to weaken, to press down, and to lessen the activity and force of, an area that is sunk below the rest." Depressed people walk around with their head hung down looking "pressed down, weakened, and sunken" just as the enemy wants them to be.

DETERMINING ITS ROOTS AND DISCOVERING IT IN ME

Depression can arise from one event, but it is far more likely to be the result of a build-up of problems and difficulties over a period of time. The loss of a job alone might not put you in depression, but the loss of a job, a recent divorce, a sick loved one, a burglary, a fallout with friends, and a physical ailment, can easily result in a state of depression. For many people, depression has become a lifestyle because of deep wounds they have developed over a long period of time. They have become professional victims of their own lives without even realizing it.

Have you experienced a build-up of problems and difficulties in your life? Are you feeling tired and alone? What about feeling angry at the unfairness and injustice you face? Have you experienced loss, broken relationships, and unresolved conflict with others? Are you feeling sorry for yourself? Would you like some relief? Most people generally know when they're in trouble emotionally. Here are some questions you can ask yourself to bring further understanding into what you are experiencing.

Do you sleep an excessive amount or too little? Are you restful or restless? Looking at your sleep patterns is one of the best gauges to tell if you are depressed or not. If you struggle to sleep, experience insomnia or restless sleep, or sleep too much, you are most likely depressed about something.

Are you angry? How much anger are you experiencing? Bob Phillips says: "It is possible to be angry without being depressed but almost impossible to be depressed without being angry. What are you angry about? Is it hurt or a loss? Who are you angry with? Are you mad with yourself, or mad at God? Are you angry about some situation in which you find yourself? You must deal with the anger to deal with the depression. Some people would rather be depressed than deal with their hurt and anger."[4]

Do you really want to get out? Acknowledging that you are *"in the pit"* (see Ps. 88:4), as David called it, must precede our next line of questioning. Some people like *"the pit"* as they enjoy the pain and the attention they receive from it. They are professional victims and don't know how to play another role. They would rather have the attention of playing the victim than be free. Jesus asked the man who had been at the pool of Bethesda for 38 years: *"Are you really in earnest about getting well?"* (John 5:6b).

What event in your life happened at that time? Knowing how long you have felt depressed is important to your further understanding and insight and brings us to our fourth line of questioning: What events have reinforced this feeling since that time? What situation, conversation, and/or conflict triggered your depressive thoughts? Many things, from emotionally charged to mundane and neutral things, can trigger a recollection of past negative experiences. These are filled with guilt, hurt, loss, and anger.

This is not uncommon or unnatural because you never truly forget all your experiences. They will often return from where you have stored them in your memory banks to haunt you and give you trouble. The more emotionally charged they are, the more they can cause strong mood changes which can lead to depression. But remember, you have a choice; you are not at their mercy. If you will acknowledge them, own them, forgive those you need to forgive, and make peace with what you cannot change, those memories can become friends. They can become a stepping-stone to growth and maturity instead of a stumbling block to depression that they have previously been.[5]

DEFEATING DEPRESSION

David discovered the solution to overcoming depression in his life. *"Hope in God and wait expectantly for Him, for I shall yet praise Him, my Help and my God"* (Ps. 42:5b).

Once you have acknowledged your problem and gained some understanding, then you must be determined to *make some decisions* in your life. Your happiness is your choice. It is not what happens *to* us but rather what happens *in* us that makes us unhappy or happy.

1. Make a decision to get out of bed and help someone else so that you can take your eyes off yourself. At a meeting, Dr. Karl Menninger was asked what a person should do if he felt a nervous breakdown coming on. The famous psychiatrist said, "Lock up your house, go across the railroad tracks, and find someone in need and do something for him."[6] As Christians, we should be strengthening, comforting, encouraging, and helping others; the added bonus is that it will help us in the process.

2. Make yourself look good, and leave the house that you have been hiding away in and have been miserable in all day. When you are out walking, lift up your head and do not let it hang down. Remember that as a child of God, you have your own *"Lifter of our Heads,"* the Holy Spirit, who is ever-ready to take us out of the miry clay we find ourselves in (see Ps. 3:3; 40:2).

3. When you are at home, put on some good Christian music that will help lift your soul. Stop watching depressing television programs like soap operas, as these will only serve to add to your depression.

4. The way to deal with disappointment is to get reappointed and become re-envisioned with the purpose and the calling God has on your life. When your despair tells you that there is no way out, remember that Jesus will make a way where there is no way (see John 14:6).

5. Discipline your spending. An undisciplined life today will cause depression tomorrow. If your spending is higher than your income, your upkeep will be your downfall. Your emotions will get you in a mess as they want instant gratification through spending and eating, etc. The flesh thinks only about today, but then you suffer the consequences tomorrow. Wisdom waits and considers tomorrow.

6. Do not take yourself and life too seriously. Decide to smile and laugh more, as the Bible says, *"A merry heart does good, like medicine"* (Prov. 17:22a NKJV).

7. Put precautions in place so you can protect and guard your heart. Do not remain passive when you realize that you've entered into the depression elevator and are going down into the pit. Resist the devil at his onset. Know how the devil can attack you and be prepared to fight him. The devil is *"like a roaring lion"* always looking for someone to devour (see 1 Pet. 5:8 NKJV). But he is a defeated foe, and *"He who is in you is greater than he who is in the world"* (1 John 4:4b NKJV).

8. The Bible says to put on a garment of praise for a spirit of heaviness, and lift up your hands to praise Him (see Isa. 61:3). Like David said: *"I will praise the Lord"* (see Ps. 146:2). It is an act of your will, and as you make a sacrifice of praise and thanksgiving, your emotions will follow. It will help to eradicate depression from your life. Instead of looking down and inward, you need to look upward to Jesus, the author and finisher of your faith, and outward to others to whom you can be a blessing.

9. Fellowship with Spirit-filled, Bible-believing people. Find yourself one of these churches instead of a social club filled with fear, doubt, and unbelief. Follow Peter and John's example who went back to *"their own company"* after being released from prison (see Acts 4:23).

The Bible gives us great and wonderful promises. Here are just a few to meditate on: John 16:33; 14:27; Isaiah 41:10, Psalm 27:13-14.

ENDNOTES

1   John McManamy, McMan's Depression and Bipolar Web: *Lincoln and his Depressions*: http://www.mcmanweb.com/article-225.htm

2. Bob Phillips, *Controlling Your Emotions Before They Control You*, (Eugene, OR: Harvest House Publishers, 1995), 54 paraphrased.

3. Ibid., 56 paraphrased.

4. Ibid., 63 paraphrased.

5. Ibid., 65-66 paraphrased.

6. Dr. Karl Menninger: http://www.menningerclinic.com/about/early-history.htm

Chapter 5

ESCAPING ENVY

SHAKESPEARE CALLED IT "THE GREEN-EYED MONSTER," but envy can be simply defined as "sorrow over another's good." It is sadness or discontent at the good fortune or success of another person, which is regarded as a hindrance to our own good and that the other's success somehow lessens our stature, value, or worth. Envy forms when we believe and feel that the other person's advantages or possessions diminish us. Envy not only sorrows at another's prosperity, but it joys over their hurt as well.

FORMS OF ENVY

Possessions

Primarily, another's wealth and prosperity produce these emotions in us. The psalmist says: *"For I was envious of the foolish and arrogant when I saw the prosperity of the wicked"* (Ps. 73:3). God does not have a problem with us having possessions as long as we are first seeking the Kingdom of God and His righteousness. While we may believe that possessions have the power to change our lives, in reality they give us only a moment of elation before we need to move on to our next "material conquest" to achieve the same emotional high.

The Favor and Attention of a Parent

How envious have you been of a brother or sister because of the attention and favor your parents have given them? Many sibling relationships have been strained from childhood well into adulthood because of this, real or perceived, favor and attention from one or both parents. The Bible tells us how envy and jealousy between siblings can lead to destruction. *"But when his brothers saw that their father loved {Joseph} more...they hated him..."* (Gen. 37:4). It finally led to this end result: *"And the patriarchs...boiling with envy and hatred and anger, sold Joseph into slavery"* (Acts 7:9a).

Favor and Position With God

The first murder in the Bible happened in the first family and between siblings because of envy and jealousy (see Gen. 4:8). Cain lusted for the recognition and honor from God that was given to Abel, and his envy led to anger and murder. The author of these emotions is the enemy. *"{And} be not like Cain who {took his nature and got his motivation} from the evil one and slew his brother"* (1 John 3:12a).

No good fruit will come from allowing envy to take hold of our hearts: "[When] *they grew envious of Moses and of Aaron...the earth opened up and swallowed* [them]" (Ps. 106:16-17a NIV). Do not be quick to resent or envy the privileges of leadership, especially if you don't know the price they have paid to get there. Spiritual gifts are given by the Holy Spirit as He wills, not as any man wills (see 1 Cor. 12:11). Their gifting does not diminish, distract, or devalue you in any way. Envy causes confused thinking, and the Word says, *"For where you have envy and selfish ambition, there you will find disorder and every evil practice"* (James 3:16 NIV).

Popularity

King Saul hated it when David, the underling, became more popular than him; his lust for popularity then gave birth to envy and jealousy. These emotions turned to hatred and Saul attempted several times to murder David. This story leaves us without any doubt as to the serious nature of these emotions and how they rend us vulnerable to the devil. *"And the women responded...saying, Saul has slain thousands, and David his ten thousands. And Saul was very angry, for the saying displeased him; and...he eyed David from that day forward. The next day an evil spirit...came mightily upon Saul"* (1 Sam. 18:7-10a).

Jesus was hated by the religious leaders because of His popularity with the people. *"For* [Pilate] *knew that it was because of envy that they had handed Him* [Jesus] *over to him"* (Matt. 27:18).

The apostle Paul also suffered as the result of envy and jealousy: *"But when the Jews saw the crowds, filled with envy and jealousy they contradicted what was said by*

Paul and talked abusively {reviling and slandering him}" (Acts 13:45). But don't think that blowing out someone else's candles will make yours shine brighter.

A TREE OF GOOD AND EVIL

The Bible often refers to us being like a tree with roots, branches, and fruit (see Ps. 1:3; Jer. 17:8). Let's first examine the roots of the tree of envy before we look at the other parts.

The Roots of Envy

While envy manifests itself externally, it originates in the heart (see Luke 6:45). *"As* [a man] *thinks in his heart, so is he"* (Prov. 23:7a). Therefore, we need to change what is in our hearts (the roots) in order to change the fruit (our behavior, attitude, emotions) that we produce. But how did these rotten roots of envy and jealousy get into our hearts in the first place?

Part of the answer lies in the fact that we live in such a performance-oriented world. From our earliest years and memories, we were required (and pushed) to compete with our siblings and our friends for our parents' love, attention, and approval. This then extended to the classroom where we continued to compete for our teacher's approval, attention, and acceptance. To not compete meant failure and rejection; to succeed meant wonderful rewards such as feelings of worth, value, and acceptance.

Acceptance of ourselves was therefore based in external and visible things. We felt accepted for what we could do rather than in who we were. The more we had and could do, the more acceptable we were. "If you *have* and *can do*, and I *don't* and *can't*, then you are of more worth and value than me." Envy and jealousy are therefore easily birthed in our hearts when we feel diminished and devalued by others' success, popularity, and advantages.

Our worth is also tied in with *others*. We feel special only if certain others love us and if we feel we "belong" to them as a special friend or spouse. Fear is at the root of the extreme possessiveness in our relationships because if I lose you, I lose my worth and value. This distorted picture also translates into our relationship with God. We feel we have to earn His approval and His acceptance. In any case, our worth is neither in Him nor in His love for us, but in external things and other people.

The Branches of Envy

The branches of our tree are comparison and competition. It's hard not to compete and compare as we are constantly surrounded with celebrity in the media and are urged to compete for material and external success. Ecclesiastes says: *"And I saw that all labor and all achievement spring from man's envy of his neighbor. This too is meaningless, a chasing after the wind"* (Eccl. 4:4 NIV). We need to bring balance to our lives. Yes, we must strive for excellence, challenging ourselves to follow our dreams. Pushing ourselves to unlock all our potential can bring joy, fulfillment, and achievement in our lives if our motive is not to compete or compare ourselves with those around us.

However, if we do good works in order just to be envied by others, it is pure vanity. Richard Armour wrote, "If there is a sin more deadly than envy, it is being pleased at being envied."[1] *"Let us not become conceited* [arrogant], *provoking one another, envying one another"* (Gal. 5:26 NKJV). Our conversations can become boastful and competitive as we try to convince others and ourselves of our own worthiness and success. We are reminded again: *"But if you have bitter envy and self-seeking in your hearts, do not boast..."* (James 3:14 NKJV).

The Rotten Fruit

The bad fruit that results from the rotten roots of envy and jealousy include the following:

1. Poor and failing health (see Prov. 14:30).

2. Broken relationships (see James 4:1-2).

3. Great unhappiness and pain (see Gen. 4:12).

4. Bitterness (see Prov. 13:5).

5. Physical aggression and violence (see Prov. 6:34).

6. An unsteady spiritual walk (see Ps. 73:2-3).

7. Spiritual death (see Gal. 5:21; Rom. 1:29-32).

UPROOTING THE EVIL TREE

1. We must become *"rooted deep in love and founded securely on love {of God}"* (Eph. 3:17b). God loves us and has fearfully and wonderfully made us. Therefore we are an original and unique creation. We must rejoice and celebrate how and who God has made us. Only then can we fulfill our unique destiny and calling. John Wesley said, "To wish to be the person you aren't is to waste the person you are."[2]

2. Once we are convinced of His love for us, we must walk in love toward others. The Bible says that *"love never is envious nor boils over with jealousy"* (1 Cor 13:4b) and it *"rejoices when right and truth prevail"*

(1 Cor. 13:4-6). Our neighbor's good can be the object of love or the object of envy, which is contrary to love. Love rejoices in our neighbor's good, while envy grieves over it. Envy and jealousy lead us to sorrow instead of rejoicing. The Bible tells us to love, bless, do good, and pray for our enemies, for that is God's will for us (see Matt. 5:44 NKJV).

3. Essential in the uprooting of our tree is to learn to be content. The apostle Paul said it was something that he learned: *"Not that I speak in regard to need, for I have learned in whatever state I am, to be content"* (Phil. 4:11 NKJV). We too can learn this contentment that is an inner peace and joy not based in outside or external circumstances but rather a trust and faith in God. The Bible describes it as "a sense of inward sufficiency" (see 1 Tim. 6:6). It is a faith—not that circumstances won't come against me or that all my problems will disappear—but a faith in His Word that He strengthens me and that He has a good future and destiny planned for me (see Heb. 13:5; Jer. 29:11).

4. It is not wrong to have desires and dreams, but James tells us that first and foremost our heart motives must be right with God: *"Seek first the kingdom of God and His righteousness, and all these things shall be added to you"* (Matt. 6:33 NKJV). Then, ask in faith believing that *"He is the rewarder of those who...diligently seek Him"* (Heb. 11:6b). As a Christian, you are an heir to all that is Christ's; just believe that He wants to bless you super-abundantly and He will (see Eph. 3:20).

5. Be a praiser. Focus on God, not on your circumstances or on other people; and *"in everything give thanks"* (1 Thess. 5:18a). When you give thanks, you continue to look at your blessings and not at your lack. A grateful heart is so full of thanksgiving that there is no room left for anything else.

ENDNOTES

1. Richard Armour: http://www.cfdevotionals.org/devpg98/de980105.htm
2. John Wesley: http://www.christophers.org/nn422.html

Chapter 6

FACING FEAR

WHAT IS FEAR?

FEAR IS ONE OF OUR MOST BASIC EMOTIONS, and it is also the first emotion mentioned in the Bible (see Gen. 3:7-10). Today, the fear of something evil happening overwhelms many people who give an inordinate amount of attention to the media, which constantly report bad news and violence happening around the world.

The root word of fear is *phobos*, meaning, "to flight and to run away from," thus we have the word *phobia*. There are over 200 categorized fears called phobias. The majority of us may be confident and strong in several areas but fearful and cowardly in others. These fears are real and frightening to the people who have them; therefore, to belittle their fears is to not fully understand the torment and bondage they cause in that person's life. Franklin D. Roosevelt in his first inaugural address at the height of the Great Depression, declared "Let me assert my firm belief that the only thing we have to fear is fear itself—nameless, unreasoning, unjustified terror which paralyzes needed efforts to convert retreat into advance."[1]

Fear produces a whole range of rotten fruit, starting with feelings of being overwhelmed, anguished, and anxious. It affects victims' self-esteem, leaving them with no self-confidence so that they become timid and shy. They feel miserable and discouraged, as well as depressed, lonely, sad, scared, worried, frantic, and nervous. Their minds are troubled and confused, and they will often feel a combination of all these and other emotions.

How do all these emotions with fear at their root affect our bodies? Physical symptoms include sweating, muscle tension, neck ache and backache, headaches, abdominal pain, ulcers, and nausea. With enough thoughts of fear, you can experience diarrhea, high blood pressure, rapid heartbeat (i.e. heart palpitations), and sexual problems.

The physical effect fear has on the body starts when a message is sent to the brain telling it that the person is in danger and under stress. The brain in turn causes the glands in the body to release adrenalin. Adrenalin empowers us for "fight or flight"—that is, for self-preservation and protection. Fear can have a positive effect on our lives when it helps us to protect ourselves and helps to preserve life. The adrenalin that our bodies produce because of fear will help us function to our peak performance as it sharpens our senses. But when the brain constantly receives too many messages of danger and fear, it will release too much adrenalin, which will have a negative overload effect on our bodies.

Vines Commentary defines *fear* as being "that which is caused by the intimidation of adversaries." Whenever we want to do something new, or move forward and upward with our lives, fear rushes up to intimidate us; when we want to confront those who are violating our rights, fear once again rushes up in our face to intimidate us. Its desire is to stop us and hold us back; fear steals all our self-confidence and as we bow our knee to it, it makes us a coward. When we want to testify about our faith, or speak to someone and give them an encouraging word, fear won't let us. Fear causes us to become man-pleasers instead of God-pleasers. Fear clouds our mind and causes small molehills to become overwhelming mountains; it confuses us into seeing large shadows for minor things.

William A. Ward said, "Worry is faith in the negative, trust in the unpleasant, assurance of disaster, and belief in defeat. It is a magnet hat attracts negative conditions; faith is a more powerful force that creates positive circumstances. Worry is wasting today's time to clutter up tomorrow's opportunities with yesterday's troubles."[2] Fear will be the darkroom where all your negatives get developed.

The Scriptures give us a great and precious promise: *"For God did not give us a spirit of timidity (of cowardice, of craven and cringing and fawning fear), but {He has given us a spirit} of power and of love and of calm and well-balanced mind..."* (2 Tim. 1:7).

The Bible also says, *"For {the Spirit which} you have now received {is} not a spirit of slavery to put you once more in bondage to fear..."* (Rom. 8:15). We once were "slaves to fear," but through the Spirit of God, we can now be released and set free.

The Bible is also full of a "good fear" when it refers to the worshipful, reverential respect and awe of God. Fearing the Lord is not only good for our health, but it also prolongs our lives (see Prov. 10:27). This type of godly fear includes a good respect as it produces an obedience and submission to those who are rightfully in authority over us.

BREAKING FEAR

We must understand and be willing to recognize that we will spend much of our lives making mistakes. Roosevelt said, "He who makes no mistakes makes no progress."[3] We are conceited if we think we can go through our lives making no mistakes; they are guaranteed to happen in our lives so we must learn not to personalize them. Make sure that you know your failure does not make *you* a failure.

Many people think that they must eliminate all fear from their lives. This is not true, for you can never totally avoid fear. A lot of people suffer from condemnation because they feel there's something wrong with them when they are afraid. It would be more accurate to say there's something wrong with you if you don't feel fear when faced with new challenges or breaking old strongholds over your life. The most important key to overcoming fear is to realize that when you feel the fear, you press through and do it anyway. In other words: *do it afraid!*

Many people in the Bible were given the instruction to "fear not." In fact, there are amazingly 365 "fear not's" in the Bible. One for every day of the year! It would appear God knew that there would be something to fear and we would need some reassurance. Joshua learned that he didn't have to be like Moses; he just had to do what God said, know that God was with him, and that God would make up the difference. Likewise, Jesus went about doing good and healing those oppressed by the devil because *"God was with Him"* (Acts 10:38b).

Our mistake is not in feeling afraid, but it is allowing the fear to stop us. The Bible never says, "Shake not, sweat not, tremble not, and do not let your knees knock together." But rather it says, "Fear not." Remember, fear is phobos meaning, "flight, to run away from." The Bible warns us *do not be frightened or intimidated...by your opponents and adversaries* (Phil. 1:28a).

God is telling you that fear will come out to fight against you, but do not be worried. Do not let fear control your life. You must make a decision based on God's Word, not on your fear, which is just a feeling. One difference between a defeated and a victorious Christian is the latter does not allow their emotions of fear to control them. Do things because you are determined to overcome your fears in your life; do them because you want freedom more than anything else and because you want to grow in your walk with God.

Do it afraid regardless of the mistakes you'll make, remembering that "no mistakes, no progress." The irrational nature of fear that clouds our minds, making molehills into mountains, ensures that the thought of doing something is far worse than the reality of it. For example, most people handle confrontation really well when it is unplanned or when they are taken by surprise. Yet the thought of planning such a confrontation can be frightening, to the point of almost tormenting them. Interestingly, 99 percent of all we fear concerning the future never even comes to pass.

To escape the bondage of fear into freedom, you must go through some pain. This pain will include facing the truth, confronting the issues, and overcoming fear. Gaining more and more freedom by "doing it afraid" is what it will take for you to break the strongholds of fear in your life.

So when will I not feel fear? The only answer to that is—in Heaven someday. As long as you want growth and freedom, you'll have fear. The good news is—as you grow in competence and confidence, it will get easier. Fear's ability to control you will diminish until it eventually loses its power and effect over you altogether. The Bible says, *"Do not, therefore, fling away your fearless confidence, for it carries a great and glorious compensation of reward"* (Heb. 10:35).

CONFESSION OF FEAR

One of the keys to overcoming fear is to recognize it as sin, because anything not of faith is sin. Fear is the opposite of faith. Faith is the realm that God works in, and fear is the realm that the devil works in. It is placing self above God; it is placing man's opinion over God's Word. Again, the Bible tells us that *"if he draws back and shrinks in fear, My soul has no delight or pleasure in him"* (Heb. 10:38b).

Fear is sin. It wants to control everything in your life as opposed to trusting God to whom you have given your life. It is sin because I am choosing not to believe His Word that says: *"Though I walk through the valley of the shadow of death, I will fear or dread no evil, for You are with me"* (Ps. 23:4a); and *"The Lord is my Light and my Salvation—whom shall I fear or dread? The Lord is the Refuge and Stronghold of my life—of whom shall I be afraid?"* (Ps. 27:1). God constantly reassures us in His Word that He will never fail us, leave us, forsake us, or let us down" (see Heb. 13:5).

Fear does not generate concern for others but spends a lot of time and energy thinking about self. Fear makes you the center of attention. Self-pity and a fearful victim-mentality lead to inward thinking and selfishness, whereas the healthiest people emotionally are those who have given their lives over to helping other people. *"Let no one then seek his own good and advantage and profit, but {rather} each one of the other {let him seek the welfare of his neighbor}"* (1 Cor. 10:24).

My first reaction to fear must be of repentance and once again recommitting the control of my life to God. In this way I hand over all my fears to Him and choose to believe that He is with me and He loves me. His love in me and for me casts out all my fear (see 1 John 4:18). As I speak the Word of God over my life, it renews my mind and has the power to transform me.

A Biblical Promise

> My God, El Shaddai, the One who is more than enough, is in control of my life. He is well able to deliver me from all my fears, from all my troubles, and from all my enemies. He is my light and my salvation. He is my refuge and the stronghold of my life, so of whom shall I be afraid? Even though I may walk through the valley of the shadow of death, I need fear no evil for He is with me. My God will never fail me nor leave me without support; He will not in any degree leave me helpless nor let me down, nor even relax His hold on me. I know that I can do all things through Him who strengthens me; and as I trust Him, all things will work out for good in my life. I believe that He who started this good work in me is well able to bring it to completion. And I know my life is secure because He has thoughts of peace and not evil for me, and He has a hope and a good future planned for me.

Endnotes

1. Roosevelt: http://www.multied.com/FDRinaug.txt

2. William A. Ward: http://www.moveahead1.com/articles/article_details.asp?id=30

3. Roosevelt: http://www.moveahead1.com/articles/article_details.asp?id=30

Chapter 7

GOVERNING GUILT

WHAT IS GUILT?

THE AMERICAN HERITAGE DICTIONARY SAYS that *guilt* is "the remorseful awareness of having done something wrong." Guilt is a feeling of regret about what one has done or not done. The difference between guilt and shame is guilt concerns your behavior, whereas shame is the feeling of being unworthy, inadequate, or defective. Shame is expressed in the belief that "there is something wrong with me." In other words, when I feel guilt, I feel I have made a mistake; when I feel shame, I feel I *am* a mistake!

HEALTHY GUILT VERSUS CRIPPLING GUILT

Healthy guilt says our conscience is functioning and allows us to look back long enough to learn a lesson. If we never reviewed our mistakes, we would continue to make them. The still, small voice of the conscience lets us know when we have done something wrong. Martin Luther wrote, "I am more afraid of my own heart than the pope and all his cardinals. I have a pope within me, the great pope, self."[1] Acts 24:16 says, *"I myself always strive to have a conscience without offense toward God and men"* (NKJV).

We can, however, get stuck in overwhelming and crippling guilt regarding our past failures, mistakes, and sins when we continue to review them in our minds and live backward. We torment ourselves with images of what could have, would have, or should have been! Instead of our focus being on what we can do now, we make ourselves victims of past regret and remorse. This crippling guilt is destructive. *"For godly sorrow produces repentance that leading to salvation, not to be regretted; but the sorrow of the world produces death"* (2 Cor. 7:10 NKJV).

Saul is a good example of what not to do. When confronted by Samuel about his sin, he lied, spoke half-truths, attempted to spiritualize his sin, excused his behavior, and finally blamed the people. The Bible tells us, *"And the Lord regretted that He had made Saul king over Israel"* (1 Sam. 15:35b NKJV).

David likewise sinned before God but was declared a man after God's own heart. These two kings teach us that our past sin never determines God's blessing in our lives. Your heart's reaction makes the difference. Unlike Saul, David's immediate reaction when confronted by his sin was repentance, with no excuse, justification, or blame upon others. *"I have sinned against the Lord"* (2 Sam. 12:13a NKJV). Because of this attitude, God put away his sin. The story still leaves us with David overwhelmed and flooded by the guilt of his sin.

PSALM 51

This Psalm provides us with an insight into David's heart and how he finally overcame the guilt he experienced.

> Verse 1:*"Have mercy upon me, O God, according to Your steadfast love."*
>
> David acknowledges the nature and character of God. Vital to David's success and emotional deliverance is his understanding of the nature of our wonderful heavenly Father. God's mercy is not according to anything that we've done or not done, but is according to who He is. Our Lord is *"slow to anger and plenteous in mercy..."* (Ps. 103:8b).
>
> Verse 2: *"Cleanse me from my sin."*
>
> This is David's prayer request because he knows only God can make him clean. Only God can make him feel good again. David also realizes that although the forgiveness is instant, it will take time for his emotions to line up with what God has done. We walk by faith and receive His forgiveness by faith, so don't rely on your feelings to tell you whether you're forgiven or not. Your feelings will eventually fall in line with your decision to live and walk by faith.
>
> Verse 3: *"I acknowledge my transgressions, and my sin is ever before me."*
>
> This is David's honest confession and open acknowledgment of his sins. The power of sin is in its secrecy; whereas, bringing these past

sins out into the open through confession, together with prayer, causes them to lose their grip on our lives.

Verse 4: *"Against You, You only, have I sinned."*

There is no healing in blaming others. Excuses and justifying yourself will never bring about the healing, growth, and change you desire. Accepting full responsibility for where and how you messed up and throwing yourself on His mercy as David did is the only way to be "made wholly pure again."

Verse 5: *"Behold, I was brought forth in iniquity."*

David acknowledges his sinful human nature. Our sinful nature will always be antagonistic to the things of God. You cannot be conceited and think that you should not have failed, messed up, or sinned as *"all have sinned and are falling short of the honor and glory of God"* (Rom. 3:23).

Verse 6: *"You desire truth in the inner being."*

There are times you will need to look at yourself in the mirror and face the truth of who you are and what you have done. God can make the difference only when you face the truth and admit your problem.

Verses 7-8: *"Wash me, and I shall be whiter than snow."*

David knew how to receive His forgiveness and to forgive himself. If we cannot receive what Jesus died to give us, we reject His grace and deny the power of the Cross in our lives.

MY PERSONAL TESTIMONY: I know what it is like to withhold forgiveness as I struggled for many years to forgive myself after I had an abortion.

After Michael and I were first married we wanted to start a family, but because a German measles epidemic was spreading and I was working as a social worker and coming into contact with people who had this disease, we decided that before becoming pregnant, I should first have the inoculation against the disease. Two months after I had the inoculation I became pregnant. The specialists emphasized that it was necessary to have an abortion because the baby would be seriously deformed. At the time, we both had finished Bible school and were part of a Bible-preaching, faith-filled church; we considered ourselves to be strong believers who could or would believe God for anything. When this crisis occurred, we were unable and too immature to deal with it. At about seven weeks into the pregnancy, I went ahead and had the medical abortion. Immediately afterward, I felt devastated that I had gone against everything I believed in. I was angry and disappointed with myself. I felt I had failed and let myself and God down. I felt like a hypocrite. I could understand that God in his infinite love and compassion for me could forgive me, but I could not and would not forgive myself. I felt I did not deserve to be forgiven and therefore withheld it from myself for eight years. In this time I had my two beautiful children and immigrated to England, yet spiritually I was not growing as I should have. Finally, one day, while talking to a pastor friend, I realized I had no right to withhold forgiveness from myself as I was not my own. I had been bought with a price, the precious blood of Jesus Christ. I was finally able to receive the forgiveness Jesus died to give me. My feelings also fell in line and I received healing for my hurting, bitter heart. As I tell the story now, the sting of the memory has gone; it is though it happened to someone else. I know how important it is to be able to forgive yourself. If you have not forgiven yourself, it is time for you to let it drop and accept what Christ did on the Cross for you as a complete and thorough work.

Verse 9: *"Hide Your face from my sins."*

When God "hides His face" and "blots out our sins," He remembers them no more. The Bible reminds us that He removes them *"as far as the east is from the west"* (Ps. 103:12a). God's forgiveness brings us to the place where the misery has been pulled out of the memory, just like the sting from an insect bite. God not only heals the emotional trauma but promises to *"not remember the sins of your youth* [the past]*"* (Ps. 25:7).

Verse 10: *"Create in me a clean heart."*

A *"clean heart"* is a pure and clear conscience. It is something to be greatly valued, and it's the prize worth pressing in for. Someone once said, "There's no pillow as soft as a clear conscience." Benjamin Franklin wrote, "A good conscience is a continuous Christmas."[2]

Verses 11-12: *"Cast me not away from Your presence."*

The Holy Spirit is our helper, strengthener, and comforter. He is also the first person we offend and grieve when we sin. We see David's desperate desire not to lose the presence of God in his life. God will never leave you nor forsake you, but He will withdraw His presence from you when you have unconfessed sin in your life.

Verse 13: *"I teach transgressors Your ways."*

Once you have been to God in prayer and dealt with your sin and guilt and received your deliverance, *then* He wants you to take your eyes off yourself and go and help someone else. Whatever God does in you He also wants to do through you.

Verses 14-15: *"Lord, open my lips, and my mouth shall show forth Your praise."*

David knew the power of praise, and he knew how to give a sacrifice of thanksgiving. My flesh may not feel like praising God, but I choose to praise God by an act of my will. Praise puts my problems into their proper context—my problems are small and God is great.

Verse 16: *"For You delight not in sacrifice."*

Do not be tempted to give God a "burnt offering" of self-sacrificial and self-righteous works. This verse paraphrased says: "There is nothing more I can do; if there were, I would do it." Guilt will want to make you do things you feel you must so that you can pay for your sin and "feel the pain" of your mistake and failure! This thinking is religious and unscriptural. Jesus gave the final blood sacrifice, and His blood is more than sufficient to pay for all your sins.

Verse 17: *"My sacrifice to God is a broken spirit and a contrite heart."*

God is a God of hearts, and He requires first and foremost that our hearts be right before Him.

Verse 18: *"Rebuild the walls."*

We too can trust God to repair any damage done by our sin. David's prayer to God—"do good" and "rebuild"—is that there would be no further delay to God's plans. There will be some things that you cannot change, you cannot undo, and you cannot repair; but for those things, you can trust Him to turn all things for good in your life.

Verse 19: *"Then will You delight in the sacrifices of righteousness."*

Doing works of righteousness and justice needs to be out of a pure heart motive rather than out of a guilty conscience and in an attempt to get Him to love and forgive you. The Bible says, *"There is therefore now no condemnation to those who are in Christ Jesus, who do not walk according to the flesh, but according to the Spirit"* (Rom. 8:1 NKJV).

ENDNOTES

1. Martin Luther: http://www.quotationvault.com/author/Martin_Luther
2. Ben Franklin:http://www.fellowshipbiblechurch.info/sermons/011605

Chapter 8

HANDLING HURT

THE OXFORD ENGLISH DICTIONARY DEFINES *hurt* as "to wound or to damage" or "the cause of pain, injury or distress." We live in a world where the hurting, broken, and damaged have reached epidemic proportions. Hurt is not prejudiced; it attacks people of all ages, backgrounds, religions, and cultures.

An emotionally wounded person is like an apple that has been dropped. You don't necessarily notice the bruise immediately, but after a while, a dark spot appears and later rots the whole apple. That apple, if left in a basket of apples, will eventually affect the other apples. Hurt can affect the whole personality and eventually affect others. Hurting people hurt people and bruised people bruise people. *"The spirit of a man will sustain him in sickness, but who can bear a broken spirit?"* (Prov. 18:14 NKJV).

It is a fallacy that time heals. When a loved one dies, the intensity of the pain may lessen after a certain amount of time has expired, but if time truly healed, we all would become whole; we would never need the balm of Gilead. The fact is, only God can heal a broken heart. *"He heals the brokenhearted and binds up their wounds"* (Ps. 147:3 NKJV).

Jesus' ministry was primarily about preaching and healing. *"The Spirit of the Lord {is} upon Me, because He has anointed Me to preach the good news to the poor; He has sent Me to announce release to the captives and recovery of sight to the blind, to send forth as delivered those who are oppressed {who are downtrodden, **bruised**, crushed, and broken down by calamity}"* (Luke 4:18-19, emphasis added). The word "bruised" in this Scripture means "to be broken into pieces." Jesus came to make whole those who are hurting.

HURTFUL WORDS

Understanding is the doorway to deliverance, and we need to first understand that we are hurt emotionally by the negative, unkind, and hurtful words of others. Job, talking about his friends, said, *"How long will you torment my soul, and break me in pieces with words?"* (Job 19:2 NKJV). It's a fallacy that "sticks and stones can break my bones, but words will never hurt me." Words emotionally damage the soul.

When my husband, Michael, at the age of 7 overheard his singing teacher tell someone that he had a terrible singing voice, he didn't sing again for the next 20 years of his life. Those insensitive words robbed him of freedom that he should have had in that area of his life. Thankfully, through His walk with God, he received the healing he needed. Unfortunately, the list of similar incidents is endless, and many never receive healing and wholeness in their hearts and minds.

When a person believes the negative words spoken over them, the emotional wounding becomes far worse; and when lodged in the heart, they speak it out over themselves. "I'm stupid; I'm dumb; I'm ugly; I'm worthless; I'm useless." We believe whatever we hear often enough. *"The words of a talebearer are like tasty trifles, and they go down into the inmost body"* (Prov. 26:22 NKJV). We have the power of life and death in our words, and they can either lift us up or bring death and destruction (see Prov. 18:21). Those who have been the victim of someone's unkind words should be very cautious of what they do with these words, so that they do not also carelessly use them to wound others.

HURTING OTHERS AND HURTING OURSELVES

Both unintentional and intentional hurt are considered sin. *"For if you forgive men their trespasses, your heavenly Father will also forgive you. But if you do not forgive men their trespasses, neither will your Father forgive your trespasses"* (Matt. 6:14-15 NKJV).

It is usually "significant others" who cause the most damage in our lives. David said, *"Even my own familiar friend in whom I trusted, who ate my bread, has lifted up his heel against me"* (Ps. 41:9 NKJV). One of Jesus' closest disciples, Peter, denied Him, and Judas betrayed Him. So don't be surprised when you're let down by those close to you. To keep this in perspective, remember that you have let others down too. It takes maturity to understand that our close relationships will disappoint and hurt us (see Matt. 16:23).

We can also hurt ourselves by our own sinful behavior. Consider this verse about David: *"And David's heart condemned him after he had numbered the people. So David said to the Lord, 'I have sinned greatly in what I have done'"* (2 Sam. 24:10a NKJV).

OUR MAN-MADE DEFENSE MECHANISMS AND REACTIONS

Inner Vows or Promises

This includes a strong inner determination and decision that people make to ensure that no one will hurt, control, and abuse them again. These promises create self-made, invisible, but *real walls* around our hearts. When we withdraw behind these walls, we create another kind of pain for ourselves in that we cannot give or receive any love. We may feel we have protected ourselves, but in reality, we have just imprisoned ourselves in loneliness and isolation. Consequently, we prevent ourselves from enjoying closeness and intimacy in our relationships. Fear of being hurt again prevents us from trusting enough to come out from behind our walls to build close, intimate relationships. If we live behind these walls long enough, we probably won't realize how to break free, even if we desperately want to.

Pretending Not to Care

Scar tissue on our heart caused by previous hurts provokes us to bitterness, and we say things we may not really mean like, "Who needs you anyway?"; "I'll make it on my own"; or "You don't bother me!" No one wants to have a relationship with a cold, hardhearted, distant, and bitter person. The resulting distrust and suspicion do not contribute toward a healthy relationship but result in further rejection and hurt. Men are often guilty of pretending that everything is okay in order to keep their "macho image" together. They find it difficult to acknowledge to themselves that they're hurting or share their pain with anyone close to them, which results in even more conflict and distance in their relationships.

Treating All Relationships as a "Training Exercise"

In this instance, our unspoken attitude is "let me teach and train you so that you know exactly how to love me and not hurt me." Acting as the victim, these people will manipulate you into pandering to all their insecurities, rejection, and hurts. Couples will often try to change and mold each other to accommodate their own insecurities, which happens to be a recipe for an unhappy relationship filled with frustration and strife. God doesn't want anyone pandering to our hurts, but rather wants us to overcome our difficulties, deal with the issues, and receive healing.

It is hard work for your loved ones to be constantly "tip-toeing" around you, trying to accommodate you as "the victim." It is exhausting, emotionally draining, and difficult to tolerate; so, ultimately there is more rejection and more hurt as the relationship breaks down. When we attempt to change others to suit our own agenda, then God will not participate. He will only help you when you trust and obey Him.

The Attitude of Aggression

The attitude of aggression says, "I'll make you more miserable than you have made me." Hurt is at the root of a bully, whether it's a child or adult. People who blame everyone and everything else for the problems in their lives do so because it takes the attention off them and they do not have to face the hurtful truth and consequent pain of their own lives and actions (see Eph. 4:29-31 NKJV).

We can spend the whole day seemingly peaceful, but the minute someone does something wrong, our aggressive, intolerant, impatient, and unkind persona shows up. My husband and I use the expression, "Stop biting my head off!" Perhaps all day long we have been brooding over some offense, feeling upset or hurt, and finally the "pressure cooker" explodes and boils over at the first, poor, unsuspecting victim. As we brood over the hurt for a long time, our thought life infects our moods and causes us to "ooze" out all forms of negative emotional reactions like anger, bitterness, and aggression. Remember, approximately 75 percent of our expressed anger is not related to our present circumstances. Although it is so easy to become angry, the Word instructs us not to sin in our anger, whether we are justified in doing so or not (see Eph. 4:26-27).

THE GODLY RESPONSE

Repent

If you are the offender, then you need to repent. *"Look at my affliction and my pain, and forgive all my sins"* (Ps. 25:18 NKJV). We need to repent for our sin and take responsibility for our sinful reactions instead of blaming everyone else. Playing the blame-game causes us to become victims of others and of our past. But God has not called us to be victims, but victors and masters of our own destiny. Repent for trying to handle the hurt in your own way, using ineffective and sinful coping mechanisms.

Forgive

If you have been the victim, then you need to forgive. Forgiveness is not waiting for people to come to you to apologize for hurting you. Realize that a large percentage of the people who have hurt you would not know what you were talking about if you confronted them on the matter. Even if they did acknowledge what had happened, they would most likely feel justified in what they did, which would fill you with even more discord, strife, and hurt in that relationship.

This situation must be balanced with wisdom, to know when it is right to confront someone with the truth as opposed to knowing when to overlook the offense. It is usually best to *"speak truth with* [your] *neighbor"* (see Eph. 4:25 NKJV) when the main purpose is to bring reconciliation and understanding, not for payback or to get revenge.

Forgiveness acknowledges that *"vengeance is God's"* (see Rom. 12:17-21 NKJV). A sure way of detecting unforgiveness is to determine if you have the attitude that "they must pay for what they did to me" in your heart.

Forgiveness does not keep a record of another's wrongs so that you can retell them to prove to others what your offenders did to you (see 1 Cor. 13:5 NKJV). By refusing to punish them for what they did to you, you truly release God to deal with the matter. God does not go around telling everyone what you have done wrong; neither should you discuss how others have sinned against you.

Forgiveness does not deny, ignore, or excuse what another has done; but acknowledges the hurt, the pain, and the sin; and chooses, in light of all the offenses, to extend mercy anyway, just as God has shown mercy to us. Showing mercy will help you recover (see Prov. 11:17 NKJV).

Forgiveness is not necessarily reconciliation. It takes two people to agree, make up, and be reconciled. Releasing forgiveness is an act of my will and something that takes place in my heart regardless if reconciliation has taken place or not. My forgiveness is not dependant on anyone else.

Forgiveness is not first receiving forgiveness from God before we extend it to others. Rather, we can only receive daily help and forgiveness from God *once* we have forgiven others (see Matt. 6:11-12 NKJV).

Forgiveness is not an optional extra. God's Word does not merely suggest it to us, but rather commands us to forgive (see Matt. 6:14-15).

Chapter 9

IDENTIFYING INSECURITY

WEBSTER'S DICTIONARY DEFINES *insecurity* as being "uncertain, unstable and lacking in confidence." It is also defined as being "unsure, shaky and unsound." Do you perhaps become *uncertain* when people disapprove of you? Or do you feel *unstable* when their opinion of what you should do differs from yours? Maybe you feel *unsure* and *shaky* about who you are? Is your worth and value as a person easily undermined by someone else? Do you perhaps lack self-confidence to step out and do or say something when you know you want to? If you said yes to any of these questions, then you are most likely struggling with insecurity.

Insecurity has reached epidemic proportions, and it's no surprise that relationships are struggling and failing with insecure people relating to insecure people.

The Greek word for *secure* means "having full command"; "to be strong"; "to rule and to be without anxiety and free from care." This is God's best for us; it's what Jesus died to give us. *"No weapon that is formed against you shall prosper, and every tongue that shall rise against you in judgement you shall show to be in the wrong. This {peace, righteousness, **security** triumph over opposition} is the heritage of the servants of the Lord..."* (Isa. 54:17, emphasis added).

If you excuse your insecurities, you will make little or no progress in your life toward freedom. Your overwhelming love for God, in addition to your absolute hatred and scorn of the devil and how he can manipulate and torment you must propel you to attack the insecurities in your life. Only your personal and vital relationship with Jesus can bring about your permanent and complete healing.

WHAT CAUSES INSECURITY?

The story of Mephibosheth in the Bible outlines what continues to happen today with those who are struggling with insecurity. At the young age of 5, Mephibosheth was dropped while in the arms of someone he trusted, and as a result, he was crippled (see 2 Sam. 4:4). Many years later, David finds Mephibosheth in a place called Lodebar meaning, "a desert, a wilderness, a place of shame and a city of despair" and brings him to the palace and seats him at the king's table (see 2 Sam. 9:5). But Mephibosheth not only has a physical problem, but an emotional one as well. He says to David, *"What is your servant that you should look upon such a dead dog as I am?"* (2 Sam. 9:8b, see also verses 7-9). When someone we trust hurts us, our perception of who we are becomes distorted, and we see ourselves as worthless dogs, impossible to love, and unworthy of God's favor. How can I crawl up into the lap of a heavenly Father and call Him "Daddy"? Will He not also eventually see the ugly, unlovable side of me and abandon and reject me as others have"? This distorted view of ourselves, based on the encounters and experiences we have had with people who have wounded us along the way, also distorts our concept of who God is.

However, God has made a covenant with you and will bring you out of the place of despair and shame, just as He did for Mephibosheth. He will change the false concepts and "stinking thinking" you have of yourself and of Him, and bring you to a place of joy and peace.

THE EIGHT REACTIONS OF INSECURITY

Insecurity Causes Us to Perceive Things Incorrectly

Insecurity draws the wrong conclusions, resulting in mental torment and suffering. We respond in ways God never intended. You may believe that someone is rejecting you because they are acting in an unloving and uncaring way about your "obvious" hurt and upset. But in reality, you may not have communicated your problem to them, and they know nothing about your pain. You may believe that as you walk into a room, people are talking about you; but in reality, they haven't even noticed you are there. Or perhaps you have sinned and believe that God is angry with you, but God will never reject you and you are forever accepted in the beloved (see Eph. 1:6).

Insecure people give others what they themselves would like to receive, but when what is given is not accepted (often because others don't have the same needs), the insecure are crushed emotionally by the perceived rejection. It's like giving someone else a drink when you are thirsty.

This often happens between couples during stressful times, who give each other what they each feel they would like to receive in that situation. The husband doesn't comfort and console his wife but withdraws, because isolation is what he desires and is how he copes. His lack of involvement is proof to her that he is unloving and uncaring. When the wife tries to comfort and console him, he gets annoyed with what he perceives to be interference and rejects her help. Men usually want to be left alone to deal with issues in their time. Yet both scenarios cause the insecure to deal with further rejection and pain, which leads to more strife and breakdown of the relationship.

The Insecure Cannot Receive Love

The insecure do not love themselves; thus, they reason that no one else can love them. Their "stinking thinking" questions why anyone would want something that has no real value, resulting in the distrust of anyone who says they love them. The insecure also believe that the person professing to love them would not really love them if they saw the "real them." Love is therefore deflected and rejection is expected. They often reject the other person first so they can avoid more pain; consequently, they are unable to sustain loving, healthy, lasting relationships. This proves that they are unlovable and have no worth to others and to God. The insecure believe that they have not earned God's love and therefore He cannot love them.

Insecurity Is Suffocating

On the one hand, the insecure person rejects those around them, but on the other hand, he places impossible demands on those he loves and who are trying to love him. Ultimately, he is looking to those he loves to do what only God can do for him, which is to give him a sense of self-worth. His need of attention and affection is insatiable, and he requires endless feedback, encouragement, and affirmation. And in turn, he lavishes those he loves with extraordinary attention, such as gifts, cards, phone calls, etc. He appears to be buying friendship and love by giving out of his need to be loved.

The relationship becomes imbalanced as the insecure person becomes overbearing with his attention and affection. Few relationships can sustain this pressure over a period of time; hence, the cycle of hurt and rejection repeats in his life. The insecure person cannot understand why he is being rejected, especially when he has been so "giving and loving." The answer lies in the fact that the people he professes to love feel pressured and emotionally suffocated. The insecure person needs to realize that he is giving to meet his own needs, not the other person's needs.

The Insecure Are People Pleasers

The Bible says, *"For they loved the approval and the praise and the glory that come from men {instead of and} more than the glory that comes from God. {They valued their credit with men more than their credit with God}"* (John 12:43). There is no freedom for the insecure person to follow God because his desperate need for self-worth causes him to be constantly concerned about what others think of him. People pleasers are vulnerable to manipulation by others. Although we will never know what others truly think, the insecure think the worst. But indeed, what can another person's thoughts really do to us? They will think what they want to about us no matter what we do!

It is important to understand that as long as our self-worth is based on what others think about us, we will be vulnerable to emotional torment and rejection that keeps us from the will of God for our lives. The Bible asks us, *"Now am I trying to win the favor of men, or God? Do I seek to please men? If I were still seeking popularity with men, I should not be a bond servant of Christ"* (Gal. 1:10).

Insecurity Is Manipulative

Although the insecure allow others to easily manipulate them, they in turn can also be very controlling. Their need for attention and affirmation is usually so great they will do anything to get it, including tantrums, sulking, tears, and lectures. They feel the person who loves them must be taught how not to hurt them and how to accommodate their hang-ups and insecurities. Their justification is that no one has experienced as much suffering as they have had to endure.

Manipulators may appear to be strong, but they live with a lot of fear and are therefore weak in character. Actually, strong people are able to let others be free, while controllers, insecure about themselves and their decisions, attempt to persuade everyone else to do the same thing as they do. The insecure think of themselves and want everyone else's attention to be on them too. Instead of meeting the needs of others, they want everyone to meet their needs.

The Insecure Struggle With Effective Communication

The insecure cannot accept that anyone would disagree with them, correct them, or be honest with them, because their self-worth is in what they do and not who they are. When anyone disagrees with them, it is perceived that their self-worth is being attacked and they are being rejected. The same person, will often correct those around them. They are usually opinionated people who are quick to tell anyone off for hurting or offending them. Insecurity says, "I don't really want your opinion; don't be honest with me, just tell me I'm right!" Confrontation and correction are scary things for an insecure person.

Disagreement, however, is part of a healthy relationship. We can disagree and still love and respect people. Secure people take correction from God. *"A fool despises...correction"* (Prov. 15:5a); but *"The ear that listens to the reproof {that leads to or gives} life will remain among the wise"* (Prov. 15:31); and *"Hear counsel, receive instruction, and accept correction, that you may be wise in the time to come"* (Prov. 19:20). Correction is not rejection!

Insecurity Uses Things on the Outside to Feel Good on the Inside

The insecure use the world's standards of money, status, and power to give them a sense of self-worth. Security, cannot be in these things, because they are neither sure nor dependable and will not give you the self-worth and value you are longing for.

When our worth is dependant upon external things, then we need constant reinforcements to make us feel good. Therefore, when we fail to achieve these things, we feel worthless, but when we succeed, we become arrogant and full of pride. Many successful men and women who have achieved great things are miserable because they have been driven and tormented along the path to success, becoming workaholics to prove that they have value and worth. Insecurity and pride are both consumed with self, the one thinking too little of oneself, the other too highly. The balanced view is that we are unique, special, and of great worth and value; but apart from Christ we can do nothing!

Insecurity Drives Into Futile Perfectionism

Perfectionism not only places a heavy burden on the insecure but also on those around them as they have unrealistic and idealistic expectations. This inevitably leads to disappointment and broken relationships. Perfectionism is a hard task master driving you to work harder, yet never enjoying the achievements you've accomplished, never feeling good enough, and always feeling unacceptable. Perfectionism steals your joy and your freedom as its goal is always unattainable.

The insecure try to earn their self-worth by being perfect. However, the acceptance, approval, and the unconditional love of God is already theirs through Christ. The biblical definition of perfection is "to grow to complete maturity." This pressing toward the mark is a lifelong process. God says that He will *"…show Himself strong in behalf of those whose hearts are blameless toward Him"* (2 Chron. 16:9a). As long as you are pressing toward God and wanting His progress in your life, He will count you as perfect while you are making the trip.

GOD'S UNCONDITIONAL LOVE

Before we try to improve any of our relationships, we must first come to love ourselves and experience the unconditional love of God. As God's children, we need to start seeing ourselves through His eyes.

The good news is that with God our insecurity does not have to be a permanent condition: *"Yet amid all these things we are more than conquerors and gain a surpassing victory through Him Who loved us"* (Rom. 8:37).

Get rooted *"deep in love and founded securely on love"* (Eph. 3:17b). Get your mind renewed to God's love that will always aggress toward us. *"{And the Lord answered} Can a woman forget her nursing child, that she should not have compassion on the son of her womb? Yes, they may forget, yet I will not forget you"* (Isa. 49:15).

We need to stop trying to perfect ourselves and instead spend our lives pleasing God. Stop trying to do what only God can do: *"…the God of all grace…will Himself complete and make you what you ought to be, establish and ground you securely, and strengthen, and settle you"* (1 Pet. 5:10).

A mature Christian tries his best and believes God for the rest. He knows that even at his very best he will still make mistakes. He knows living under self-hatred, condemnation, guilt, and self-rejection will not help him live a holier life. And a mature Christian knows that if he presses toward his God-given right of security that God will heal his emotional handicap. Surrender to Him by humbly accepting and receiving all Jesus died to give you (see James 1:21).

Chapter 10

JUDGMENTAL OR JOYFUL

THE OXFORD ENGLISH DICTIONARY DEFINES *judging* as "to form an opinion about, to estimate, to act as a judge, to conclude and to consider." The word *judgment* is defined as "the critical faculty, discernment, good sense and opinion."

From these definitions, we see that judgment is the useful ability to determine or discern between right and wrong. Making judgments is a necessary part of daily life. We are constantly required to form opinions, to estimate and draw conclusions, and to make many decisions. These decisions can be as small as deciding where to shop to greater decisions involving disciplining children.

PERVERTED FOR EVIL

Aside from making good and healthy everyday judgments, problems can occur when we use our ability to judge in areas that we do not have the license or the freedom to judge. It is easy to step over into sin and begin to pass judgment on other people, feeling we are entitled to an opinion. Before long, our attitude can deteriorate and we find ourselves critical and judgmental toward everything and everyone.

We must remember that the sin nature that operates through the flesh is antagonistic and opposed to anything that is godly, righteous, and of the Spirit. Many times we allow the enemy to take our God-given ability to judge and pervert it for evil with the intention of causing harm to others. We would do well to remember the following saying when tempted to be judgmental: "Don't look down on others; only God is that high up."

Without realizing it, we often make assumptions about people according to their outward appearance or by the way they talk. A good example to follow is the Samaritans who offer training to volunteers, teaching them to listen to people without jumping to conclusions or making judgments too quickly that could most likely be incorrect.[1] They advise to first listen and then ask key questions to obtain as many facts as possible so that an assessment can be made regarding the individual and his situation without any personal prejudice or bias.

WHAT YOU SOW, YOU WILL REAP

To set ourselves on high and assume the authority of judge and jury over someone else's life is to be arrogant and to consider ourselves more highly than we ought. This type of behavior has a destructive and damaging affect on our relationships and ultimately produces negative results in the life of the person who judges. The Scriptures are very clear concerning this subject, and Jesus warns in Matthew:

> *Do not judge and criticize and condemn others, so that you may not be judged and criticized and condemned yourselves. For just as you judge and criticize and condemn others, you will be judged, criticized and condemned, and in accordance with the measure you...deal out to others, it will be dealt out again to you* (Matthew 7:1-2).

Jesus explains that the principle of sowing and reaping is at work and not to be surprised when what we mete out to others comes back to us, including judgment and criticism.

Bearing this principle in mind, we know we can also expect to receive the measure of grace and mercy that we mete out. Most of us would admit that we need an abundance of grace and mercy. Knowing this, we should be ready to give both whenever we can. To give you a simple example, whenever I drive and another driver pulls out in front of me, I smile and give them some room knowing that I often make regular driving mistakes for which I need mercy. Often, I make mistakes because I'm distracted or in too much of a hurry. Therefore, when someone else is seemingly rude when driving, I find it easy to forgive them.

BE AWARE OF THE BEAM IN YOUR OWN EYE

There are other times when we do not know ourselves very well. The disciple Peter is a classic example of someone who did not fully appreciate what he was capable of. Peter emphatically swore that he would never betray or desert Jesus; but, in the pressure of the moment, he did exactly that. Perhaps there are things you have declared in the past that you would "never do." Yet in time you have discovered yourself doing exactly the same thing you declared you wouldn't.

We are supposed to use our God-given "critical faculty" to judge our own behavior first. The problem is that we lack self-insight and, like Peter, have judged ourselves incorrectly. The Bible exhorts us to *"let every person carefully scrutinize and examine and test his own conduct and his own work"* (Gal. 6:4a). And elsewhere it says:

> *For if we searchingly examined ourselves {detect our shortcomings and recognizing our own condition}, we should not be judged and penalty decreed {by the divine judgement}. But when we {fall short and} are judged by the Lord, we are disciplined and chastened, so that we may not {finally} be condemned...with the world* (1 Corinthians 11:31-32).

It is God's divine strategy that we first sort out our own problems; then He releases us in the compassion, mercy, wisdom, and insight that we have learned, in order to help others.

> *Why do you stare from without at the very small particle that is in your brother's eye but do not become aware of and consider the beam of timber that is in your own eye? Or how can you say to your brother, Let me get the tiny particle out of your eye, when there is the beam of timber in your own eye? You hypocrite, first get the beam of timber out of your own eye, and then you will see clearly to take the tiny particle out of your brother's eye* (Matthew 7:3-5).

In the meantime, while we have so much of our own problems and troubles to deal with, we are not capable to act as a judge, as we are often blinded by our own faults and failings (the beam of timber) and therefore miscalculate others and their situations. Many times, we can be blinded by arrogance and self-righteousness. It is very convenient and prejudiced to judge ourselves according to our own heart motives while at the same time judging others according to their actions and behavior. The Book of Proverbs tells us that we are poor judges even of our own hearts:

> *Every way of a man is right in his own eyes, but the Lord weighs and tries the hearts* (Proverbs 21:2).

If we are unable to judge ourselves correctly, how will we possibly ever be good judges of others?

The most important thing we can do is to begin to judge ourselves. It is only through examining ourselves in the light of God's Word that we are able to *"expose, sift, analyze, and judge the very thoughts and purposes of the heart"* (Heb. 4:12b). We are humbled when we finally reach a place of acknowledgment of our own faults and shortcomings, an essential process we must go through before we are able to help others gently deal with the splinter in their eyes.

THE CONSEQUENCES

Nobody has been given the task to judge creation other than the Creator Himself. In the Book of Revelation, we see that all of Heaven comes to a standstill because no one can be found to open the book or scroll. Finally, the only One found worthy to open the book is Jesus, the Lion of the tribe of Judah (see Rev. 5:1-5; 6:1). Ultimately, we commit the same sin that lucifer committed by thinking we can be "like God" when we pass judgment on others. We also judge according to the individual's strength alone and do not take into account that the Master, who is God, is able to make them endure and overcome.

> *Who are you to pass judgment on and censure another's household servant?*
> *It is before his own master that he stands or falls. And he shall stand and*
> *be upheld, for the Master (the Lord) is mighty to support him and make*
> *him stand* (Romans 14:4).

In the Book of Revelation, the seals on the book that only Jesus is able to open, have to do with the judgment of the nations. Upon opening the seals, four horses are released in sequential order. This order is significant to what can happen to us today when we take the role of judging others upon ourselves.

The first horse that is released is Conquest: *"...he rode forth conquering and to conquer"* (Rev. 6:2). When people feel judged, they instinctively feel conquered and dominated by someone else's opinions. Conquest says, "I am going to take over your life in some particular area," so people respond in fear, feeling that their freedom is threatened.

The second horse released is War (see Rev. 6:3-4). One thing you must realize is that not everyone will compliantly accept your judgment. Many are likely to war with you over your pronounced judgment and opinion. When you are experiencing a lot of strife and contention in your relationships, you must ask yourself if it is because you are being judgmental and critical. Another word for *contention* is "contest." Do you always want to be heard and constantly think that you are right? Do you often fight to have the last word?

Many times, a judgmental person doesn't really feel that he's right, so it becomes essential that their opinions are always "right."

Even when we are sure that someone is wrong or God allows you to discern that something or someone is incorrect, this does not mean that you have a license to declare it to anybody. You may be discerning and accurate in your insight, but God will still not sanction your judgment over other people's lives, unless it is within a disciplinary capacity and a church setting, administered by elders and those who are spiritually mature (see 1 Cor. 4:5).

The third horse released is Famine (see Rev. 6:5-6). Famine can be the loss of all that is good, such as your peace, joy, finances, and resources.

The fourth horse to be released is Death (see Rev. 6:7-8). The last stage to occur will often be the death of a relationship, the loss of happiness, the end of a marriage, or the destruction of church harmony.

When we deem ourselves worthy to be the judge of others, we must be prepared to face the consequences. If you are suffering with strife, contention, and the loss of precious relationships in your life, you must consider whether you are releasing any "horses" through a critical and judgmental attitude. We are to judge only what God wants us to judge and to leave the rest well alone.

THE WORTHY JUDGE

The fifth and final horse to be released is the horse of God's judgment, which will be accomplished in His perfect timing (see Rev. 6:9). God is never hasty or premature. He allows the wheat and the tares to grow together so that no damage to the wheat is done when they are pulled out together (see Matt. 13:24-30).

It is noteworthy that Jesus is described in this portion of Scripture as the "Lamb of God" and not the "Lion of the tribe of Judah" as previously named. This symbolizes that He is merciful and loving even in His judgment. He wants to win us with His love and goodness (see Rom. 2:4). Our aim then is to be like Him, and to overlook the offenses, failings, and weaknesses of those around us. We are called to walk in love toward others; to be gracious, slow to anger, and quick to forgive others. If we want mercy, grace, kindness, and patience to be shown to us, we must be prepared to measure it out to others—that is the spiritual law.

It is a joyful day when we realize that we are released from being the judge, as it is only God's responsibility (see Rev. 6:10). And we can rest knowing that God will judge mercifully, justly, and righteously. We can be content, walking in freedom by taking our eyes off the evil, the wrong, the incorrect, and the unjust, and instead focus on the good, the lovely, and the praiseworthy (see Phil. 4:8). We are then content that we are in the will of God with no horses released in our lives, and gratefully leave the judging up to the only One who is worthy to judge—Jesus.

ENDNOTE

1. Samaritans, http://www.samaritans.org.uk/

Chapter 11

KALEIDOSCOPE OF EMOTIONS

GOD HAS BLESSED US WITH THE CAPACITY TO experience and demonstrate a broad range of wonderful emotions. As His unique creation, we have been given a soul, which comprises the mind, the will, and the emotions (see Gen. 1:26). When we give our lives to Jesus, we surrender our souls to Him and that means surrendering our emotions too.

Many Christians think that their goal is to rid themselves of all negative emotions in order to become more Christ-like. This is neither possible nor healthy. Rather, God requires that we master our emotions and learn to express them in a constructive and righteous way. We do not deny our emotions' existence, but in Christ we deny them the right to rule us. Our goal is to be like Jesus who experienced the full range of human emotion, yet did not sin (see Heb. 4:15).

According to the Webster's English Dictionary, *emotion* is a "complex, usually strong response involving physiological changes as a preparation to action," or simply put "an internal motion that moves us in a direction or causes us to move away."

Ultimately, God wants us less concerned and aware of our own feelings and needs and more sensitive to the feelings and needs of others. As followers of Christ, we are meant to be moved by emotions in order to show compassion and understanding to those in need. The correct purpose and use of feelings and emotion is:

...so that we may also be able to comfort (console and encourage) those who are in any kind of trouble or distress, with the comfort (consolation and encouragement) with which we ourselves are comforted (consoled and encouraged) by God (2 Corinthians 1:4).

THE NEED FOR EMOTIONAL BALANCE

Some people struggle to experience and express reasonable emotion. Often, these people are so calloused from the trials of life that they "feel" very little and are numb inside. Yet they do have feelings; they are simply unable or unwilling to express them.

The other extreme involves those who are overly emotional and who are ruled by emotion as opposed to reason. Their emotions are concerned with only what is happening at the moment. While emotion is rash and calls for immediate action, wisdom looks calmly ahead to determine how a decision will affect the future. Someone who is very emotional lives a life tossed to and fro by every feeling he or she experiences, whether the emotions are helpful and valid, or unreliable and destructive.

When we first moved to the United Kingdom, I discovered I had been controlling my emotions very carefully in an attempt to be strong for everyone. This meant I was unable to cry tears at the grief and homesickness I was experiencing even when I wanted to. Eventually, my grief came out in dreams in which I found myself sobbing over the fictitious death of a family member. At this point, I realized that I needed God to touch my heart and bring down all the walls I had erected around it. God was then able to set me free to express my emotions in a healthy way. It is also God's desire to set you free to live a healthy and emotionally balanced life.

FICKLE FEELINGS

Emotions can be fickle and unreliable. There are times when our emotions seem to support us and we feel very excited about what God is instructing us to do. We then perceive the emotional support we are feeling as confirmation of God's will for our lives. However, there are times when God's Spirit leads and guides us to do something that our emotions don't seem to support, and thus we find it difficult to do God's will. When we lack the understanding about the inconsistent nature of our feelings, the devil will use them, or the lack of them, to keep us out of the will of God. And if we continue to take counsel from fickle feelings, we will never walk consistently in victory and in the will of God.

Emotions can also lie to us. If you are insecure and walk into a room, you may instantly "feel" that everyone is talking about you, but the likelihood is that they haven't even noticed that you've arrived. If you are having an emotionally down day, it is easy to "feel" that nobody understands, appreciates, or loves you, even though this is probably false and your perceptions are incorrect. Emotions can't be trusted.

People who have suffered an abusive past may experience many emotions that cause considerable damage, including guilt, shame, loss, trauma, failure, and a host of others. When someone's soul is hurt and crippled, they often do not experience emotions in a balanced moderate way. Often, emotional responses triggered by present circumstances and relationships are actually reactions based on past brokenness. The emotional response is far too great or exaggerated to be caused solely by the current issues and often has nothing to do with the present situation at all. Hence, it is difficult to realistically understand our lives through emotions that may have been distorted by past brokenness.

CONTROLLING AND DANGEROUS EMOTIONS

Emotions operate through the flesh. The Scriptures tell us that by living a life of the flesh we cater to the appetites and impulses of our carnal nature (see Rom. 8:8). This describes being "emotionally driven." The Scripture also informs us that being controlled by our emotions is never acceptable to God or pleasing to Him.

> ...because the mind of the flesh {with its carnal thoughts and purposes} is hostile to God, for it does not submit itself to God's Law; indeed it cannot (Romans 8:7).

The Bible clearly teaches us that the flesh and the spirit are opposed to one another. This means that we cannot be led by our emotions and led by the Holy Spirit at the same time. Whether we realize it or not, when we choose to allow our emotions to rule over us, we have made a choice not to be led by the Spirit of God.

Feeling and experiencing negative emotions such as anger, frustration, and jealousy does not mean that you have sinned or that they are ruling you. It is your reaction to those feelings and your consequent behavior that determines whether you sin or not. For example, the Bible says "when angry, do not sin" (Eph. 4:26a). It doesn't say it is wrong to feel anger. What it means is that we are not to download our aggression, passion, and temper onto someone else, but rather restrain our anger, be assertive, and speak the truth in love to the relevant person.

The story of Cain and Abel in Genesis shows us how dangerous it is when we let our emotions control us. When Cain became angry and jealous of his brother, God warned him that *"sin crouches at your door; its desire is for you, but you must master it"* (Gen. 4:7b).

God warned Cain to master his emotions, because if he didn't, God knew they would cause him to sin. Neither Abel nor God were Cain's real problem; his uncontrolled emotions were. Cain's feelings were hurt and bruised, and in his anger and hurt, he wanted to retaliate. What he needed, rather, was self-control in order to be able to walk in forgiveness toward his brother and God. If he had been able to do this, he would have mastered his emotions; but unfortunately, he allowed his emotions to overwhelm him, and he acted on them and murdered his brother.

Our uncontrolled emotions not only have the power to determine the outcome of particular situations but can also impact the direction our lives will take. Cain's sin resulted in a lifetime of painful isolation and wandering in the desert. When our emotions rule, they remove our ability to plan our future or decide our destiny. For instance, how many of us have had an argument with someone close, neglected to exercise self-control, and allowed our emotions to determine the direction and outcome of that argument?

In his letter to the Corinthian church, the apostle Paul declared the Corinthians to be un-spiritual, fleshly, and impulsive (see 1 Cor. 3:3). He did not have an issue with them experiencing "ordinary impulses" (or emotions), but rather that they were acting impulsively and thereby living under emotional control. An impulsive person lives by every whim or fancy of the flesh; their decisions are based on emotion rather than logic or reason.

MASTERING OUR EMOTIONS

Living by Principle

As we have discussed, negative emotions can cause you to make bad decisions that can lead to sin. Making firm decisions in advance concerning your life ensures you have a plan to follow so that your emotions don't have an opportunity to leap in.

When the will of God is obvious and apparent, make sure that you make decisions in advance and be firmly committed to obey God, so that you don't easily fall into a tempting situation. Without having established a principled decision, you are more likely to react emotionally in the heat of the moment rather than be spiritually led.

For example:

- Decide before you go to bed at night to wake up 15 minutes earlier in the morning to spend time with God. Otherwise, when your alarm clock rings, you will merely press the snooze button and go back to sleep.

- Decide before you go out shopping exactly what you are going to buy according to your budget so that you are not tempted to buy anything on impulse.

- Decide before you go out to eat that you are living a disciplined lifestyle and make a conscious decision to not eat more than the amount you have previously set.

- Decide in advance exactly how you will respond to a person or situation that usually makes you react in anger, frustration, or irritation. Practice if necessary!

If you are emotionally driven, it may be something so ingrained within your flesh that nothing less than your best effort will change it.

Renewing Your Mind

Our thought processes, whether sound and wise, or flippant and foolish, dictate our emotions. Our thought processes, therefore, are the key in controlling our emotions. If we practice "stinking thinking," our thought processes will not line up with the Word of God. Our emotions, relying on our thoughts for information, cannot distinguish between falsity and reality. A good example might be when you can't find something that is precious to you. Your mind will imagine that you might never find it, or it may become suspicious that someone has stolen it. Your emotions then respond to your thoughts. In this case, you begin to worry, despair, and even get angry. Then, later on, you discover the lost item, exactly where you last put it. You realize it had never been lost, yet your emotions experienced the loss as though it were real. In actuality, they responded to what your thoughts told them.

Your "will" implements whatever your mind agrees with. If your mind is un-renewed to the Word of God, then it will agree with your flesh; then your flesh will inevitably win. But once your mind starts learning the Word of God, it begins to agree with the Spirit, and you will stop being controlled by your flesh.

There are several ways you can fight the battle for your mind. First, the Bible says to take captive every thought that exalts itself above the knowledge of God (see 2 Cor. 10:5). Many of our thoughts are lies from the enemy that we have not resisted. These lies often stir up destructive and ungodly emotions. Thoughts such as, "I'm no good"; "I'm worthless"; and "I'm a failure" can encourage negative emotions such as discouragement, dismay, and despondency. Negative emotions such as these can cause a physiological response where our body releases chemicals that contribute to disorders that result in the need for medication. The Bible tells us that thoughts have a tremendous impact on not only how we behave but also who we become (see Prov. 23:7).

Meditating on Scripture as often as possible will fill your mind with the Word of God and produce the results you are looking for (see Ps. 1:2). This is definitely the better alternative to thinking and reasoning according to our fleshly senses.

> *Now the mind of the flesh {which is sense and reason without the Holy Spirit} is death* (Romans 8:6a).

The mind of the flesh reasons and justifies sin, often producing thoughts such as, "I am allowed to slander them because of what they have done to me"; and "I know I've been depressed but I can't help it"; and "You would also worry and complain if you had my problems."

The Scripture goes on to say that the *"mind of the {Holy} Spirit is life and {soul} peace..."* (Rom. 8:6b).

Here are a few confessions you can start with:

- I can do all things through Christ who strengthens me (see Phil. 4:13).
- I am accepted in the Beloved (see Eph. 1:6).
- I am a chosen generation, a royal priesthood, a holy nation, God's own special people (see 1 Pet. 2:9).
- I do not have a spirit of fear but of power, love, and a sound mind (see 2 Tim. 1:7).
- Nothing shall by any means harm me (see Luke 10:19).
- He will never fail me nor forsake me (see Heb. 13:5).

Making Wise Decisions

Sometimes it can be difficult to know whether what we are "feeling" is from God or our emotions. The following three points should help safeguard you when faced with making a decision:

1. Ask yourself if you are making the decision based on emotion such as hurt, insecurity, and jealousy, or according to the Word of God.

2. Always submit your emotion to wisdom. If your feeling would cause you to do something foolish and unwise, it is unlikely to be from God. Make sure you get counsel.

3. Wait! The final test is to wait, because emotions always want us to be hasty. Impulse never wants to consider tomorrow, always now. Wait until you understand the whole picture. When in doubt, don't react to anything. Wait until you have a clear answer before taking a step you'll regret.

Chapter 12

LOST IN LONELINESS

MANKIND MADE FOR RELATIONSHIP

SINCE THE BEGINNING OF TIME, THE FATHER, SON, and Holy Spirit have had relationship with one another. Then God created man in His own image and likeness (see Gen. 1:26-28 NKJV). God created us to have relationship with Him and at the same time built in us a deep desire and need for companionship, fellowship, and relationship with others.

We discover that although a man named Adam walked with God in the Garden of Eden, God recognized that Adam was still "alone."

> *It is not good (sufficient, satisfactory) that the man should be alone; I will make him a helper meet (suitable, adapted, complementary) for him* (Genesis 2:18b).

God saw that mankind needed companionship in addition to his relationship with Him. And because no animal or other living creature was found to be a suitable mate for Adam, God created Eve (see Gen. 2:20-23).

God did not intend for human begins to be alone in this world. Consequently, when people live without human contact, intimacy, or connection, they experience the pain of loneliness, isolation, and disconnection.

LONELINESS, SOLITUDE, AND LONESOMENESS

Loneliness is not solitude, lonesomeness, or even feeling forlorn, but is an inner feeling of emotional isolation that can occur even in a crowd. In its severity, it is a feeling of being unwanted, unneeded, and unnecessary. It is also a painful emotional feeling of being disconnected, cut off, or isolated from the rest of the world.

Thus, loneliness is an inner feeling that has no direct relation to physical proximity to others. Some people are not lonely when they're alone, and others are lonely within a crowd. A Jewish proverb describes loneliness as "eating into the soul." Sister Teresa of Calcutta said, "Loneliness and the feeling of being uncared for and unwanted are the greatest poverty."[1] In contrast to soul prosperity that the Bible speaks about (see 3 John 2), loneliness is a poverty-stricken soul.

All different types of people experience loneliness:

- A child feels lonely when his parents are too busy to spend time with him.

- An adolescent feels lonely when she is not accepted by her peers and is being misunderstood by her parents.

- A mother with young children feels lonely when she is too busy to have her own needs for companionship met.

- A spouse can feel lonely when communication is poor and intimacy needs are not being met. (Note: Being married or living with a family is not an automatic safeguard against loneliness.)

- Someone who loses a loved one through death or divorce can experience terrible loneliness.

- Someone who is isolated through illness suffers just the same.

- The elderly who are cut off from their families and whose friends have passed away often suffer acute loneliness.

David was considered a man after God's own heart and communed with God regularly, and wrote hundreds of psalms, yet he too suffered from the despair of loneliness from time to time. He describes the despair and hopelessness he felt:

> *I am like a melancholy pelican or vulture of the wilderness; I am like a {desolate} owl of the waste places. I am sleepless and lie awake {mourning}, like a bereaved sparrow alone on the housetop* (Psalm 102:6-7).

For the person who does not know God, the depth and despair of loneliness can be tragic.

Loneliness is the feeling that we have no one to talk to and no one who understands our deepest concerns and needs. Loneliness provokes a vicious negative cycle of despair as if there is nothing to live for; hence, the victim shies away from the very social contact and support he or she needs to overcome.

Solitude is different from loneliness. Solitude is a physical isolation that is often self-imposed and for a purpose. Solitude is good for us; it is aloneness by choice and for the purpose of prayer, meditation, reflection, or to read, draw, or write. We all need solitude from time to time as it enriches and energizes us, whereas the effect of loneliness causes the opposite. It detracts and debilitates us. Solitude brings victory; loneliness is defeat.

Lonesomeness is an altogether different issue. Everyone experiences lonesomeness when they are away from their loved ones for a period of time. It is painful but not nearly as debilitating as loneliness because the person knows the pain will come to an end. This is very similar to social loneliness, which is brought on by changes such as moving away, going to college, or changing jobs. A vacuum is created, as the familiar, comfortable support systems are gone, and we often feel disconnected as though we don't belong—but this is usually only for a specific time. As we make a determined effort to meet new people, rebuild our relationships, become familiar with our new surroundings, or as we reunite with our loved ones, the feeling subsides.

Severely lonely people who constantly or regularly feel disconnected or left out, often don't know how to approach or contact others socially. They fear rejection so they don't attempt to make friends or develop relationships. These people may smile or tell you they are fine, but they are hurting inside.

The presence of many people is no protection for them against loneliness, and crowds can often make their sense of isolation worse. If they walk the streets, go into restaurants, or go to public places and see people having a good time with family and friends, their own pain increases. It is similar to sick people who feel worse when they see healthy people enjoying themselves. Lonely people thus withdraw even more.

THE CAUSES OF LONELINESS

There may be one root cause or several causes behind our loneliness. Ask yourself the following questions:

- Is your loneliness because of a communication problem? Often, people who are lonely not only struggle to communicate their feelings, but they also struggle to understand the feelings of others.

- Do you feel inadequate? People who feel inadequate are often lonely because they don't like themselves. They therefore presume that others don't like them either and thus they isolate themselves.

- Is insecurity one of the major contributing factors to your loneliness? Insecure people struggle to give themselves to relationships as it takes a sense of security to reach out and develop relationships.

- Perhaps hidden hostility and bitterness are the causes for your loneliness? The hostile person is angry at others which prevents anyone from getting too close through their negative attitude.

- Is your loneliness a result of your hurting? Lonely people may have been wounded earlier in life, and the memory of this pain causes them to keep their distance. They are afraid of being hurt again, so they hide behind protective walls, which unfortunately also become their prison.

- Is fear keeping you disconnected and isolated from others? Another major cause of loneliness is fear—fear of getting hurt, fear of rejection, fear of not measuring up, fear of losing a loved one, or fear of failure. Perhaps the pain was so great at having lost a loved one that there is fear of losing someone again; consequently, you have chosen not to draw close to anyone else.

SELF-PITY

As I have previously mentioned, there are many acceptable and reasonable situations in which people might feel and experience loneliness, from death to divorce to poor parenting to bad communication in a marriage. Within these situations, most people will experience self-pity from time to time. However, there is a turning point where the person can choose to move on to recovery, or he can choose the path of self-pity, guaranteeing additional pain.

Prolonged self-pity produces many problems for the sufferer as it holds them a victim of their own circumstances. The person who pities himself is one who feels sorry for himself and is self-centered and selfish. This self-pity automatically turns to envy toward those who have more and can do more. Instead of being grateful for what they have, they sit around feeling sorry for themselves because of what they don't have.

Remember, loneliness is introspective in nature, and a lonely person thinks that no one cares about him. And because no one likes to hang around someone sulking in their own pity, the initial loneliness is then exasperated by the self-pity. This truth may be hard to receive if you have a problem with self-pity, and it is even more difficult to tell someone you know who has the problem. *"Faithful are the wounds of a friend, but the kisses of an enemy are deceitful"* (Prov. 27:6 NKJV).

THE CURE

When we suffer from loneliness, it is an indication that our relationship with God and our relationship with people need some work and help. And there is no one better qualified to help us than the Holy Spirit.

Our Relationship With God

Many people "feel" that God is far away from them, but He is only as far away as you allow your feelings to dictate to you that He is. Instead, choose to believe the Word of God rather than your feelings:

> *The Lord is close to those who are of a broken heart and saves such as are crushed with sorrow for sin and are humbly and thoroughly penitent* (Psalm 34:18).

> *{God} Himself has said, I will not in any way fail you nor give you up nor leave you without support. {I will} not, {I will} not, {I will} not in any degree leave you helpless nor forsake nor let {you} down (relax My hold on you)! {Assuredly not!}* (Hebrews 13:5b).

> *God is faithful (reliable, trustworthy, and therefore ever true to His promise, and He can be depended on); by Him you were called into companionship and participation with His Son, Jesus Christ our Lord* (1 Corinthians 1:9).

When we practice His presence in our lives, the Holy Spirit comes alongside us to help. The Holy Spirit is the Comforter, Counselor, Helper, Intercessor, Advocate, Strengthener, and Standby (see John 14:26). If you are experiencing loneliness, you are most likely unaware of the One who is always with us and everywhere. When we allow Him, He will transform our loneliness into solitude so that we can enjoy *"fellowship (the communion and sharing together and participation) in the Holy Spirit..."* (2 Cor. 13:14b).

Choose to Serve Rather Than Sit

Fellowshipping with God helps us to focus on Him. He is the One who is more than enough and who is always with us. This in turn gives us strength to relate to others. As prayer builds companionship with God, so serving builds companionship with others. We cannot be alone when we are busy serving others, which according to Jesus, is our highest call as Christians (see Matt. 20:25-28).

Christians who choose to serve rather than sit will not suffer from loneliness. The Scriptures say that two are better than one because they have a good result for their work (see Eccl. 4:9-12). You may be 90 years old and widowed but not overcome by loneliness because you're reaching out and serving others, visiting the sick, elderly, and needy. A psychologist once said there are three steps to overcoming loneliness:

Step 1: Get involved with people.

Step 2: Get involved with people.

Step 3: Get involved with people.

As we become active and push ourselves to step out of our isolation, God will help us get connected with people, which will help us to step outside our own problems and pain and give us a place in this world.

As you become a friend, you will gain friends. The purpose of these friendships will not only be to help you overcome the loneliness, but you will also gain friends who will push you to grow and serve and give more than you do. Only a life of self-emptying can bring a life of self-fulfillment! You are needed, necessary, and so vital to the Body of Christ. There are many churches that are desperate for helpers, volunteers, and servants. If you don't know in what areas you would like to serve or how to get involved, start anywhere that there's a need and God will direct you.

"Therefore, whatever you want men to do to you, do also to them" (Matt. 7:12a NKJV). If you want to be understood, start by understanding; if you want encouragement, encourage others; if you want to be listened to and valued, then become a listener and value others.

It is our duty to pass on the goodness of God. The Bible says we are to *"comfort those who are in any trouble, with the comfort with which we ourselves are comforted by God"* (2 Cor. 1:4b NKJV). The church is your family. No family is perfect, yet even imperfect families can raise healthy, normal children. No army is perfect, yet even imperfect armies can still win battles! Discontented church-hoppers who are looking for the perfect church will miss out on the incredible opportunity to get involved and connected, and enjoy the full benefit of church family life. As a church family, we are told in Scriptures to:

↪ Be devoted to one to another (see Rom. 12:10 NIV).

↪ Accept one another (see Rom. 15:7 NIV).

- Instruct one another (see Rom. 15:14 NIV).
- Have equal concern for one another (see 1 Cor. 12:25 NIV).
- Carry each other's burdens (see Gal. 6:2 NIV).
- Encourage one another (1 Thess. 5:11 NIV).
- Pray for each other (see James 5:16 NIV).
- Offer hospitality to one another (see 1 Pet. 4:9 NIV).
- Teach and admonish one another (see Col. 3:16 NIV).

Make yourself known as a servant who is vital, needed, and necessary to other people, just as Jesus is to us.

ENDNOTE

1. Sister Teresa, http://achristiancounselor.com/lonely.html

Chapter 13

MOURNING BY MORNING

GRIEF IS A NATURAL EMOTION AND A PART OF everyone's life at some time or another. Because grief is painful, many people shy away from talking about it or dealing with it. Ignorance and misconceptions about grief only serve to compound the hurt and add a further burden to those already carrying one of life's greatest pains. Thus, our purpose is to bring help and comfort to the griever by giving understanding and insight into his grief, and to educate those around him so that they become more skilled and adequate in helping.

Webster's Dictionary defines *grief* as "a heavy emotional weight resulting from loss." Although grieving includes bereavement, which is the process we go through when we have lost someone through death, grieving can also occur at the loss of anything that is precious to us, no matter how big or small. Dr. Kindah Greening says, "It is important to understand that each person's loss is as valid as the next. Never underestimate the depth of disappointment another person is feeling. It is relative to each person."[1]

MISCONCEPTIONS

Grief is not our enemy; instead, it helps us through a process of conflicting, confusing, and painful emotions toward a place of recovery. Neither is it an instantaneous healing that comes with faith and power. The Bible says, *"Blessed are those who mourn, for they shall be comforted"* (Matt. 5:4 NKJV). And the Oxford English Dictionary says that to mourn is "to grieve for loss of…." Without the mourning or grieving process, we would never be comforted.

A common religious philosophy that says grief is unacceptable has served only to compound confusion in grieving people. Through this thinking, they experience more isolation and inner frustration by trying to ignore their feelings. Constant suppression causes the griever to struggle to maintain composure as their emotions threaten to overwhelm them. Instead of having to deal with our ignorance or rejection, they need our understanding and love.

A BIBLICAL VIEW

Grief is neither negative nor a weakness because God Himself "was grieved in His heart" (Gen. 6:6b NKJV). In the Book of Isaiah, we read that Jesus was "...a Man of sorrows and acquainted with grief" (Isa. 53:3a NKJV); and in the Gospels we find Him weeping at the death of His beloved friend, Lazarus (see John 11:35 NKJV). God doesn't frown upon people who grieve, rather the Word comforts and reassures us that our grief is normal, our ally and friend.

David said, "therefore my spirit is overwhelmed within me: My heart within me is distressed" (Ps. 143:4). Jeremiah exclaimed: "Why is my pain perpetual and my wound incurable, which refuses to be healed? Will you surely be to me like an unreliable stream, as waters that fail?" (Jer. 15:18 NKJV).

When God rejected Saul as king of Israel, the prophet Samuel mourned his fall. Their relationship had been close, and Samuel was seriously disappointed. Finally, God said to him, "How long will you mourn for Saul?" (1 Sam. 16:1a NKJV). God was not opposed to Samuel's grief, but He knew that he had grieved sufficiently and wanted him to move on. It was time for him to recover and complete the task God had for him.

After Stephen had an open vision of the throne room of God and was martyred, as recorded in the Book of Acts, the devout men of his time "made great lamentation over him" (Acts 8:2b NKJV). To lament means "a passionate expression of grief." These great, spiritual men of the early Church found the need to grieve the loss of their friend and colleague, and so should anyone who finds themselves in a similar position.

First Thessalonians 4:13b (NKJV) says that we "sorrow [not] as those who have no hope." The Christian's sorrow is different from the grief of the unsaved because he has the hope that the one who has passed away has graduated to a better place and is with the Lord in Heaven (see Cor. 5:8 NKJV). Although we mourn our loss, we receive comfort and joy for what the deceased person is now experiencing. On the other hand, the unsaved, uncertain of their eternal destiny, do not have this comfort or hope.

THE GRIEF CYCLE

Dr. Kindah Greening says, "Those who are thrown into loss and the resulting grief find their pain to be enormous and at times unbearable. They feel confused, isolated, alienated, angry, guilty, extremely frustrated, relieved, and then guilty again. Blaming themselves and others, they feel they will never recover. They feel completely lost. Gaining knowledge on the grief cycle and how to handle the symptoms is thus very helpful in dealing with the emotions constructively and avoiding destructive ways of handling them."[2]

No two persons grieve exactly the same way, but the symptoms are often very similar. There is no prescribed schedule or timetable anyone should or shouldn't follow. Not everyone lives through exactly the same experience in exactly the same set order, but following general guidelines can help the griever understand that his emotions are normal, which is comforting and reassuring.

The experts agree that the sooner the pain is faced, acknowledged, and expressed, the quicker the recovery. Following are the major stages to recovery.

Denial

The first initial reaction in the shock of severe loss is denial, disbelief, and numbness. Shock is a necessary reaction in our emotional realm because it acts as a buffer so that our soul can catch its breath and steady itself. The denial that happens at this stage is good and healthy. People can slip in and out of reality and denial within a few minutes. At this point, do not mistake an attitude of denial for faith. God does give peace that passes understanding (see Phil. 4:7 NKJV), but grief must still be acknowledged and somehow expressed.

Joyce Landorf says, "We need denial but we must not linger in it. We must recognize it as one of God's most unique tools and use it. Denial is our special oxygen mask to use when the breath-taking news of death has sucked every ounce of air out of us. It facilitates our bursting lungs by giving them their first gulps of sorrow-free air. We breathe in the breath of denial and seem to maintain life. We do not need to feel guilty or judge our level of Christianity when we clutch the mask to our mouth. However, after breathing has been restored and the initial danger has passed, we need not be dependant upon it. I think God longs for us to lay down the oxygen mask of denial and with His help begin breathing into our lungs the free air of acceptance on our own."[3]

When people try to postpone or shield themselves from or even minimize their loss with prolonged denial, they simply extend the pain and delay their recovery as well. Norman Wright in *Recovering From the Losses of Life* says,

"Grieving is moving through several levels of denial. Each stage brings home the reality of the loss a bit deeper and more painfully. We accept first in our heads, then in our feelings and finally we adjust life's pattern to reflect the reality of what has occurred."[4]

Anger

When the realization of the loss has occurred, the typical reactions are questionings, angry bargaining, pleading with God, rage, envy, and resentment. The person experiencing this stage is difficult to cope with because of his emotional outbursts. His anger is projected onto others and God while blaming himself as well. As a supporter, it is important not to take this or any emotional outburst as personal. In the Gospels, Thomas' reaction to Christ's death was first of denial as he refused to talk about it; then he went off into seclusion and reacted in anger when told Jesus had risen (see John 20:24-29).

Depression

This is the next major stage, which includes behaviors and attitudes such as withdrawal from people and activities, loss of pleasure and enjoyment of life, feelings of disappointment and loneliness, physical discomfort such as aches, pains, fatigue, poor digestion, and sleep disturbance. There is a sense of great loss and regret for things previously done or left undone. Guilt and shame are also common companions at this stage. The griever must not feel ashamed by these emotions as grief can be expressed in many different ways that range from panic and fear to calmness.

Eventually, the griever will face the loss head-on but refuse to be cheered up. The griever might not want to talk as much, and at this point, nonverbal support is most helpful. These may be some of the darkest of times as the reality of their loss sinks in even further, but we know it is often the darkest before the dawn. *"Weeping may endure for a night, but joy comes in the morning"* (Ps. 30:5b NKJV).

Acceptance of the Loss

This is the final stage. The griever is no longer in denial or angry or depressed about his fate. He starts to build new relationships and develops new patterns. However, do not mistake his acceptance and positive adjustment as happiness. He may still be void of emotions, and continuing to express your support is still invaluable. This Scripture may bring comfort to him at this stage: *"We know that all things work together for good to those who love God, to those who are the called according to His purpose"* (Rom. 8:28 NKJV).

BLOCKAGES

The road through the grieving process may have blockages that prolong the pain and hinder recovery. A person may become stuck in one of stages of the grieving process with no healing or closure in sight. These include:

1. Wrong religious or cultural ideas.

2. Prolonged denial—not wanting to face the pain or minimizing and even rationalizing the loss.

3. Certain expectations from family and friends to behave normally or to recover quickly. Because of their discomfort, they pressure the griever to forget the past, even when he is not ready to.

4. Hiding in his own private world of suffering, which is encouraged by the self-pity he is experiencing. If the griever allows himself total freedom to feel sorry for himself and his circumstances, he can become unhealthily self-focused. Resisting the temptation to wallow in self-pity will help him from becoming isolated.

5. Not giving himself enough time and space, expecting too much of himself, or trying to be brave in front of everyone around him.

6. Guilt and recrimination can shut the grieving process down.

When we judge ourselves too harshly, we can become trapped in the anger and depression stages and never progress. Some people do not want to let go of the hurt because they feel it is the only thing that connects them to the person they have lost. The grieving person must give themselves permission to forgive and let go, so they can move on to acceptance and recovery.

AS THE GRIEVER

The griever must realize he should set boundaries on his grieving process. It is all right to take charge and let others know what you need and don't need at this time in your life. Norman Wright says, "This is your loss, not theirs. No one should rob you of your grief. Some may do that because they are uncomfortable."[5]

Here are some further points to consider:

1. Find someone you have confidence in and talk through your needs with them.

2. Do not expect your community in general to know or understand what you are going through. You will only be disappointed if you have unrealistic expectations.

3. Express whatever you are feeling, whenever you want to. To hold back the tears or emotions just because someone is watching will only serve to repress emotions, training them to stay underground.

4. Be aware that other members of your family might also be struggling and trying to cope with their grief. Do what you can for them; don't be so self-absorbed that you do not give them the time or space to grieve.

5. Be yourself even if your emotions are confused and disorderly.

6. Resist guilt, condemnation, and pushing your grief underground. Don't be surprised at your anger, its intensity, or misdirection. This should just be a phase or stage of the grieving process—this too will pass.

AS THE HELPER

God's instruction to us is to comfort His people (see Isa. 40:1 NKJV). Today God needs you to spread His love and comfort to those hurting with grief and pain. *"A word fitly spoken is like apples of gold in settings of silver"* (Prov. 25:11 NKJV). Many times we would like to say just the right thing, but we feel inadequate and don't know what to say; consequently, we choose to say nothing rather than cause hurt. Yet our silence and lack of involvement are perceived as rejection and lack of concern. There are some simple do's and don'ts in order to learn to become supportive and effective helpers. Twice widowed Ida Fisher, coauthor of *Widows Guide to Life,* says the three "T's" are essential to recovering from the loss of a loved one: tears, talk, and time. Other pointers are:

1. Do not rehearse a role, but be natural and sincere. Simple affection may speak louder than any words.

2. Do not withdraw. The best gift you can give them is to listen. Allow them to talk. Keeping regular contact with them through calls, cards, and remembering anniversaries are great comfort.

3. Do not compare, evaluate, correct, or criticize them or their responses. Let them talk, reflecting back with them without making any judgments. Don't be afraid of their tears, realizing they are part

of the healing process. Don't direct their conversation or distract them with jokes or other news.

4. Sympathizing, such as saying, "You will soon feel better," or "You will feel all right" is not helpful. Sympathy is patronizing; empathy, not pity, will bring comfort.

5. Don't look for sympathy for yourself.

6. Don't dominate their lives. Visit and help only when they say they want it.

7. And finally, don't forget to pray *with* them if they are willing, and *for* them when you are alone. Your prayers will make much power available to them and help them to recover (see James 5:16 NKJV).

ENDNOTES

1. Dr. Kindah Greening, *Grief: The Toothache of the Soul* (Queensland, Australia: Healing Hurting Hearts Ministry, 1997), 46.

2. Ibid., 14.

3. Joyce Landorf, *Mourning Song* (Old Tappan, NJ: Fleming H Revell Company, 1974), 63.

4. Norman Wright, *Recovering From the Losses of Life* (Grand Rapids, MI: Baker Book House Company, 1991), 54.

5. Ibid., 58.

Chapter 14

NEEDY BY NATURE

GOD, WHO GAVE US THESE SOULS, GAVE US a strict charge with them: We must maintain a holy jealousy of ourselves, and set a strict guard, accordingly, upon all the avenues of the soul; keep our hearts from doing hurt and getting hurt, from being defiled by sin and disturbed by trouble; keep them as our jewel, as our vineyard; keep a conscience void of offense; keep out bad thoughts; keep up good thoughts; keep the affections upon right objects and in due bounds. (See Proverbs 4:23 Matthew Henry's Commentary). All of this is important because "all issues flow out of the heart" determining whether we glorify God with our lives and bless others, or whether we live defeated, unhappy, and unfulfilled lives.

UNDERSTANDING BOUNDARIES

Not many of us grow up understanding much about good boundaries; setting godly boundaries helps you to protect your own heart, and confirms to you and others that you exist apart from them and that you are in control of yourself. Christians often think that when they say "no" or establish certain boundaries on their giving or their time, they are being selfish. On the contrary, setting boundaries is learning to be self-defined and a good steward of our own souls.

Boundaries simply define who you are—where you end and someone else begins. In addition, they show us what we are *not* responsible for and what is *not* part of our "property." But whether we communicate them or not, boundaries exist and will affect us. When boundaries are not communicated, visible, or exposed directly, they will be communicated indirectly in negative ways.

BOULDERS AND BACKPACKS

When considering our responsibilities, we need to examine the Scriptures: *"Bear one another's **burdens**, and so fulfill the law of Christ"* (Gal. 6:2 NKJV, emphasis added). The word "burden" here means "excess burden or burdens which are so heavy they weigh us down." These burdens are like boulders that can crush us. We shouldn't be expected to carry a boulder—a crisis or a tragedy—by ourselves.

Another Scripture says, *"For each one shall bear his own **load**"* (Gal. 6:5 NKJV, emphasis added). Everyone has responsibilities that he or she should carry. The word "load" here means "cargo or the burden of daily toil"—the everyday things we all need to do. We are able to carry a "backpack," which represents our own feelings, attitudes, and behaviors we are expected to carry; in contrast to "boulders" for which we do not have enough strength, resources, and knowledge to carry alone.

Denying ourselves so that we can do for others what they cannot do for themselves shows the sacrificial love of Christ who did for us what we could not do for ourselves. But when people confuse the "loads" that they should or should not bear, problems arise resulting in either continuous pain or irresponsibility.

"TO" AND "FOR"

These two little words are different but easily get confused to mean the same thing. I am responsible *for* myself, my own attitudes, my own emotions, and thoughts. Therefore, I am responsible to overcome whatever problem they present or represent. If I live with anger, bitterness, and hurt, I can't offer excuses saying I am not responsible for my own problems, such as "You don't know what they did to me," or "You don't know what I've been through." Perhaps you excuse your sarcasm, sulking, and moodiness, blaming your partner or family for being selfish and inconsiderate. You have made it their problem and, therefore, feel entitled to hold onto your grudge and unforgiveness. Perhaps you direct the blame for your problems and bad attitudes toward your parents. It's their fault you are bitter and hurting, which places you at their mercy, and your life's success or failure is in their control. It declares that because they broke you, they must fix you. NO! God has placed you in charge of your soul, and He holds you responsible for yourself, not others.

I am responsible *to* others. *"Let each of you look out not only for his own interests, but also for the interests of others"* (Phil. 2:4 NKJV). I am responsible to love them, but I am not responsible for their attitudes, behavior, or emotions. Your spouse is not responsible for your emotional well-being, and you are not responsible for theirs. We can't think, feel, or work through disappointment and hurt for each other; we can't even grow spiritually for each other. We are responsible, however, to love them and to care for them.

NEITHER RELUCTANTLY NOR SORROWFULLY

The Bible is clear how we should not give: **"Let each one {give} as he has made up his own mind and purposed in his heart, not reluctantly or sorrowfully or under compulsion,** *for God loves (He takes pleasure in, prizes above other things, and is unwilling to abandon or to do without) a cheerful (joyous, 'prompt to do it') giver {whose heart is in his giving}"* (2 Cor. 9:7, emphasis added).

We are told to not only be concerned about ourselves but to be generous in giving our time and resources to others. There are conditions though: *"If it is possible,* **as much as depends on you,** *live peaceably with all men"* (Rom. 12:18 NKJV, emphasis added); and *"Do not withhold good from those to whom it is due,* **when it is in the power of your hand to do so"** (Prov. 3:27 NKJV, emphasis added). Both these Scriptures communicate the same thought: We are responsible to care and help others, but within limits. God wants us to care for ourselves so we can help others without moving into crises ourselves. Be aware when you give past the love point to the resentment point. Even when it is a legitimate or valid need we may not be able to sacrifice the help for some reason. Even Jesus left the needy multitudes for His own solitude (see Matt. 14:23).

LOVE OR FEAR

True love leads to joy and blessing. If your "loving," is making you feel depressed and sorrowful, then it's probably not love. And if your giving causes you to feel resentful and angry, then your giving is not done with love, but out of guilt or fear. Maybe you are afraid of saying "no"; afraid of upsetting or making someone mad; afraid of losing their love or approval; afraid of being disconnected, abandoned, or alone. But how do we know that experiencing this kind of fear cannot be love? Because we read in the Bible, *"There is no fear in love; but perfect love casts out fear, because fear involves torment. But he who fears has not been made perfect in love"* (1 John 4:18 NKJV). We are not being loving and generous when fear is our motive. Love and fear are incompatible in our heart; we cannot give to someone having both motives.

"Yes" and "No"

The Bible warns us to *"Let your 'Yes' be 'Yes,' and your 'No,' 'No.'"* (Matt. 5:37a NKJV). Only you know what you can and want to give, and only you are responsible for drawing the line. If you do not draw it, you will quickly become resentful. Saying no is the most basic boundary-setting word. You may be moved to give to someone in need, but then that person manipulates you into giving more than you want to give. You have just gone into "over-give"; consequently, you become resentful and angry, because you are missing something you need in your own life. Or you may want more from someone else, and so you pressure them until they give in. But they do not give out of their hearts or free will, but out of compliance, and they resent you for what they give! Often people who haven't established proper boundaries do not know how to respect the boundaries of others.

We are not selfish when we take care of ourselves and say "no" to hurtful people and activities. At these times we need to be good stewards and protect God's investment in ourselves.

As a pastor, I am wary of people who won't or can't say "no" to me and other people. They are far more dangerous than those who explain why they can't do something for me. They may say "yes" to me, but then complain to others how unfair I have been to have asked anything of them. They resent me, and yet I don't have a clue what I have done wrong. They expect me to know intuitively and instinctively that they are unable or unwilling to do the task. In other words, they make me responsible for their emotions because of their fears and lack of assertiveness. Without communicating the problem and without taking responsibility for their own decisions and lives, they still want others around them to change. Remember an internal "no" nullifies an external "yes"! Wishing that the other person wouldn't want what they are asking for, doesn't work; setting limits does. Don't resent others for not stopping you when you have been over-giving.

Sowing and Reaping

"Do not be deceived, God is not mocked; for whatever a man sows, that he will also reap" (Gal. 6:7 NKJV). When we rescue those we love from the natural consequence of their sin or negative behavior, we are interrupting the natural law of sowing and reaping. Why should they change what they are doing or saying when the only consequence they are suffering is hearing you nag about their

irresponsible behavior? Only you are experiencing the pain of their lateness, rudeness, laziness, or abuse. Cloud and Townsend say, "Some people become so accustomed to others rescuing them they begin to believe their well-being is someone else's problem. They feel let down and unloved when they aren't bailed out. They fail to accept responsibility for their own lives."[1] Our behavior should always have consequences, for good or bad: *"For if you live according to the flesh you will die; but if by the Spirit you put to death the deeds of the body, you will live"* (Rom. 8:13 NKJV).

CHOICES

Throughout the Bible people are reminded of their choices and told to take responsibility for them. *"And if it seems evil to you to serve the Lord, choose for yourselves this day whom you will serve"* (Josh. 24:15a NKJV). Often we disown our choices without even realizing it and lay it on someone else with: "I had to" or "He made me," thus once again placing someone else in control and relieving us of the responsibility. Yet when we take back our choices and make them our responsibility, we will no longer wallow in our self-pity, but will instead be empowered.

We can choose to commit to something and submit ourselves to be trained in this area. But if we have not counted the cost, we will complain and act like we are a victim of the decisions of others. When the commitment starts to get too tough for us, the giving of our time and resources then become "reluctant and sorrowful." We need to go back to our original choice! Start to take responsibility for the choices you have made as you are the only one keeping yourself from making yourself happy with better choices.

SETTING LIMITS

Often we are concerned that if we set limits or boundaries, people will not respect them. But our focus then is on the wrong people—on others instead of ourselves. Second, we judge ourselves by how we respect or condemn others' boundaries. We need to treat others and their right to say "no" as we would like them to treat us. When we accept other people's freedom, we feel better about our own.

Cloud and Townsend say, "Appropriate boundaries don't control, attack or hurt anyone. They simply prevent your treasures from being taken at the wrong time. Saying no to adults who are responsible for their own needs, may cause them discomfort. They may have to look else where. But it doesn't cause injury."[2] Don't confuse *hurt* with *harm*—they are two different things. For example, when we go to the dentist, it might hurt us, but it is for our good and will not harm us. We are responsible to consider others' feelings when we set limits, but this must not stop us from doing what we need to. We are responsible *to* others, not *for* them.

Setting boundaries does not deal with or demand anything of the other person; in fact, they are not even required to respect your boundaries. The boundaries are set for what you will or will not do. Only these kinds of boundaries are enforceable—the ones we have control over ourselves and not over others. On the other hand, you give up trying to control your partner and allow them to take responsibility for their own behavior.

God is our example. He separates Himself from a misbehaving, evil, unrepentant people; and He allows us to choose how we will behave. But if we choose a sinful life, He will not be there to participate. So too it can be with us; we can't change people's behavior, but we can limit our exposure to them when they are abusive or behave badly.

ENDNOTES

1. Dr. Henry Cloud and Dr. John Townsend, *Boundaries* (Grand Rapids, MI: Zondervan Publishing House, 1992), 118.

2. Ibid., 110.

Chapter 15

OVERWHELMED OR OVERCOMING

WHO HAS NOT FELT OVERWHELMED DURING TIMES of crises in their lives? Even David, the king of Israel, often spoke about being "overwhelmed" due to circumstances brought on by himself or others (see Ps. 142:3; 55:5 NKJV). His emotions cry out in a time of crisis: *"Therefore my spirit is overwhelmed within me; my heart within me is distressed"* (Ps. 143:4 NKJV). Although he was a man after God's own heart, he still felt overwhelmed at times. However, he knew how to overcome, and so can we (see Ps. 61:2). *"Who is he who overcomes the world, but he who believes that Jesus is the Son of God?"* (1 John 5:5 NKJV).

Crisis is defined as "a point at which a change must come, either for the better or the worse; a deciding event; a time of difficulty and of anxious waiting." We usually think of crisis in a negative context, but times of crisis can be for good. In the Chinese culture, the word *crisis* means both danger and opportunity. Managed positively, a crisis can be the basis for new opportunities.

Crises are usually a result from change, and they result in change. They include job changes, family conflicts, social pressures, financial debt, marital breakdowns, and midlife frustrations. The apostle Paul optimistically describes what would constitute a crisis for many of us: *"We are hard pressed on every side, yet not crushed; we are perplexed, but not in despair; persecuted, but not forsaken; struck down, but not destroyed"* (2 Cor. 4:8-9 NKJV).

The ABC's of Emotions

UNDERSTANDING AND MANAGING A CRISIS

*No temptation has overtaken you except such as is **common to man**; but **God is faithful**, who will **not allow you to be tempted beyond what you are able**, but with the temptation will also make **the way of escape**, that you may be able to bear it* (1 Corinthians 10:13 NKJV, emphasis added).

Four points from this key Scripture teach us how to understand and manage a crisis when we are feeling overwhelmed in our lives.

Crisis Is Common to Man

Following are elements of crisis that are common to man when feeling overwhelmed.

1. *Crisis is normal, unpredictable, and not prejudiced.*

   Change and crises are normal and common to life. You are not crazy if you have problems...I'd be surprised if you didn't have them. Bad things happen to good people. You don't experience pain because you're a bad person, but because you're a person.

   "In the world you will have tribulation; but be of good cheer, I have overcome the world" (John 16:33b NKJV). Being a Christian does not exempt you from the pains of life; however, remember that you have Christ on your side, which means you don't have to go through anything alone because you have His wisdom and strength.

2. *Crisis is stressful.*

   The stress factor that accompanies some crises is what makes them seem so unbearable. While a proper amount of stress is good for us in that it stretches us and helps us to grow, excess stress causes us to become emotional, fearful, insecure, and self-centered as we worry endlessly about ourselves. Stress is tormenting and intimidating and makes us feel overwhelmed by our inadequacies and low self-worth and hinders our ability to think and act wisely.

3. *There is a desire to escape.*

   A common desire in people during a crisis is to escape. Often they want to return to simpler, quieter times. *"My heart is grievously pained within me, and the terrors of death have fallen upon me. Fear and trembling have come upon me; horror and fright have overwhelmed me. And I say, Oh, that I had wings like a dove! I would fly away and be at rest"* (Ps. 55:4-6). The crisis makes us feel trapped, like there is no way out or around, and no way of escape from the continued burden and tension. It is not uncommon for some people to have suicidal thoughts as living may seem to be more difficult than dying! Suicide (a permanent solution), however, is not the answer to just a temporary problem.

4. *There is a feeling of helplessness.*

But you are not helpless. If you submit to the Lord and His Word, He will deliver you from all your troubles and tribulations. *"Is My hand shortened at all, that it cannot redeem? Or have I no power to deliver?"* (Isa. 50:2a). Others may desire your downfall, but when you give it to God, He turns your circumstances around for good.

5. *There is a feeling of self-pity.*

We will never become powerful if we are to remain pitiful. Self-pity doesn't fight back but wants to remain the victim, accepting all the sympathy he can get. But this is a battle we must win in order to make it back to recovery and victory.

6. *Crisis involves deception.*

The devil is the accuser; however, he not only accuses us to God, but also accuses God to us. But God is not unfaithful, nor is He the source of all your problems. It is foolishness to accuse God of being the source of your hurt, harm, and failure; when He is truly the source of your escape and success.

God Is Faithful

No temptation has overtaken you except such as is common to man; but **God** *is faithful...* (1 Corinthians 10:33 NKJV, emphasis added).

1. *Faithfulness is a requirement.*

All the qualities of faithfulness are found in God. He doesn't act or feel faithful; He simply is faithful. And His faithfulness is revealed in His relationship with man. Because God is faithful, He can be trusted to account for those of us who are His children. Jesus said He would not lose any who were entrusted to Him. *"While I was with them in the world, I kept them in Your name. Those whom You gave Me I have kept; and none of them is lost except the son of perdition, that the Scripture might be fulfilled"* (John 17:12 NKJV). God is faithful to love and care for us as He promised.

2. *When we are faithless, He is still faithful.*

"If we are faithless {do not believe and are untrue to Him}, He remains true (faithful to His Word and His righteous character), for He cannot deny Himself" (2 Tim. 2:13). Dr. Ed Cole says, "When we reach the end of ourselves and think there is nothing left in us to face the circumstances of life; when we cannot see anything else that can be done to alleviate the crisis; when there is no understanding of what to do or which way to turn, the good news is GOD IS FAITHFUL!"[1] In the midst of our greatest crisis, God is faithful and He never stops working for our good (see Rom. 8:28-29).

3. *God stays the same.*

No matter what the cause of your crisis, whether job loss, marital tensions, midlife frustration, or persecution from family, and no matter what external situations have altered and changed or what inner emotions are raging, not everything has changed. God always stays the same. He is faithful to His Word and to you! He is *"the Father of lights, with whom there is no variation or shadow of turning"* (James 1:17 NKJV). He neither slumbers nor sleeps; He will not forget, lie, repent, or fail (see Ps. 121:3; Isa. 49:15; Num. 23:19; Isa. 42:4). He can be trusted totally. Your trust during a crisis should not be in your abilities, talents, emotions, circumstances, or even yourself; your trust can only be in the living God.

We Will Not Be Tested Beyond What We Are Able

*...but God is faithful, who will **not allow you to be tempted beyond what you are able**...* (1 Corinthians 10:33 NKJV, emphasis added).

God does test the hearts of man, but He does not test us with evil (see Prov. 17:3; James 1:13). In the story of Job, the enemy had divine permission from God to test him but within limits (see Job. 1:12). We trust God that He knows how much we are able to endure. Not only does He give us the ability and power to stay calm in adversity, but we have also received *"power (ability, efficiency, and might) when the Holy Spirit has come upon you"* (Acts 1:8a) to endure and overcome. To say you cannot endure is to deny that you have the Holy Spirit living inside you, and that God cannot be trusted because He has allowed the devil to take you beyond your ability, strength, and power to endure.

Acknowledging the sovereignty of God in your life will help you place your trust in Him. You will know that He is able to overrule anything and everything in your life when He wants to. Joseph is a good example of someone who had every reason and right to give up and be angry with God, but he remained faithful to his God, recognizing His sovereignty, and stayed submitted to Him.

Avoid playing the blame-game. Blaming anyone or anything else makes you the helpless victim whose life is in others' hands. Our attitude toward our situation is what leads us to our failure or success. It is not what happens to us, but rather what happens in us. Never give up. Giving up and giving in during a crisis is one of the most demoralizing decisions we can make. Facing a crisis and overcoming it can lead to great success.

The Way of Escape

*...but with the temptation will also make **the way of escape**, that you may be able to bear it* (1 Corinthians 10:13 NKJV, emphasis added).

1. *His Word.*

   In times of crisis, our greatest hope and comfort is knowing the Word of God. When we focus on God's Word, we begin to see things from His heavenly perspective and no longer from our limited earthly view.

   "If you faint in the day of adversity, your strength is small" (Prov. 24:10 NKJV). The strength to withstand adversity comes from faith (see 1 John 5:4). Faith comes from hearing, and hearing by the Word of God (see Rom. 10:17). Therefore, it is essential that between times of crises, we make the Word of God our foundation.

2. *Hearing and obeying.*

   God's provision and power are released to us only according to the level of our obedience. We must base our obedience on faith and not on emotion. Like David, our decisions may take us away from God's will, but not out of His reach. *"Now David was greatly distressed, for the people spoke of stoning him, because the soul of all the people was grieved, every man for his sons and his daughters. But David strengthened himself in the Lord his God"* (1 Sam. 30:6 NKJV).

   David made big mistakes, but he didn't look for ways to avoid reality. He confronted it in truth. Many people in trouble try to buffer themselves from the pain of their crisis by ignoring the problem. David, on the other hand, encouraged himself by recounting what God had done in his life at other times of crisis when he called upon God. He recalled the promises, Scriptures, and revelations God had given him, and found strength. And when David was ready to hear, God spoke. *"When my spirit was overwhelmed within me, then You knew my path"* (Ps. 142:3a).

"So David recovered all that the Amalekites had carried away, and David rescued his two wives. And nothing of theirs was lacking, either small or great, sons or daughters, spoil or anything which they had taken from them; David recovered all" (1 Sam. 30:18-19 NKJV). David was able to re-cover what he had lost, but first he had to get right with God.

God did not deny David in his weakness; He took care of him super-naturally. God will do the same for you. He will not deny you in your temptation as He is faithful.

3. *Going out to come back in.*

"He makes a way of escape, that you may be able to bear it." God has a pat-tern of escape, but it is not based on how we react to crises; it is not based on an escape *from* but an escape *to*! Most times, we will do any-thing we can to avoid crises, problems, punishment, correction, and other difficult issues of life that we face. But God's idea is completely different as He plans on releasing us *to* a better place. With this in mind, a crisis is not as fearful and negative an experience as we may have previously believed.

God has to empty your hand before He can fill it again. We leave the old and enter the new many times through crises. To deliver us to sal-vation, God had to deliver us from sin—from evil to righteousness. God is ultimately more interested and concerned with where we are going than where we have come from.

Let us conclude this chapter with a quote by Dr. Ed Cole:

Transition is necessary for God to take us out of where we've been and into a better place. God gave the Israelites the exodus from Egypt so He could give them the entrance into Canaan. The history of Israel serves as an example to us. God's pattern is the same for us today. If we fail to realize that God is bringing us out to deliver us into a land that is better and brighter then we will perish in a wilderness of unbelief. We can miss our "Promised Land" by miss-ing the patterns and principles of God.[2]

He goes on to say:

God's primary goal is to bring us into a close relationship with Him. God's desire for all His children is Christlikeness. To bring us into that place and position, He first brings us out, out of our old habits, wrong attitudes, sinful thoughts, and selfish actions. When we are prepared and deal with change in a godly way, we will multiply, or increase, rather than decrease. Leaving our "Egypt," waiting in the wilderness to qualify for the Promised Land and entering Canaan all create new crises, but each crisis is a step toward a better, higher, more permanent life that God wants to give us.[3]

ENDNOTES

1. Dr. Ed Cole, *Facing the Challenge of Crisis and Change* (Tulsa, OK: Albury Publishing, 1987), 22 paraphrased.

2. Ibid., 72-73 paraphrased.

3. Ibid., 73-75 paraphrased.

Chapter 16

PITIFUL OR POWERFUL

I HAVE DISCOVERED THAT GOD LIKES TO ASK SOUL-SEARCHING questions: Adam, where are you? Cain, where is your brother? Elijah, what are you doing here? And for our realization and revelation, He asks us questions too.

Following are a few soul-searching questions. Please don't answer with "Yes, but...".

Do you feel sorry for yourself in some area of your life? Do you feel the world is treating you wrong? Do you feel life gives you negative feedback or is unfair? Do you feel that others are better off than you? Do you feel that you pick up trouble, misery, and bad luck? Do you feel that people are letting you down? Do you feel imprisoned in a life of discontentment? If you have answered "yes" to any of these questions, then keep on reading.

You must exchange the feeling of self-pity for the greater purpose in your life of becoming emotionally whole and effective in God's Kingdom. Paul said, *"I...forget what lies behind and strain forward to what lies ahead, I press on toward the goal to win the...prize to which God in Christ Jesus is calling us upward"* (Phil. 3:13-14). If your goal is to have peaceful, fulfilling relationships and to enjoy emotional wholeness, then self-pity cannot be a part of your life.

VISITOR, VICTIM, OR VICTOR

How we handle life's pressures leads us to become either pitiful or powerful. Unfortunately, our natural tendency is to respond to life's difficulties with

self-pity, and the common misconception is to believe that we should succumb to it. Two people struggling with the same terrible pain live through it
with different attitudes—one with bitterness, anger, and self-pity, playing the
blame-game, which in turn, feeds discontentment; and the other with a positive and determined attitude to get on with life and leave the past behind.

The visitor indulges in self-pity less regularly than the victim; and because
he manages to control it, the danger of this hidden emotion is rarely notice-
able to himself or others.

Others who have made self-pity part of their personalities and have perfected
the art of feeling sorry for themselves, enlisting the attention and sympathies of
those around them, can be described as the "classic victim." Both the visitor and
the victim feel they deserve to wallow in this emotion, but for their own emotional well-being, they need to choose to move on and become victorious. Healing and restoration is your choice and responsibility, not anyone else's.

Pity Versus Self-pity

"As a father pities his children, so the Lord pities those who fear Him" (Ps. 103:13
NKJV). Translators use the word "pity" here to mean "compassion," and the
Oxford English Dictionary defines it as "sorrow for another's suffering." Compassion means "to move a person to action on behalf of someone else." Pity or
compassion is never used to define feeling sorry for ourselves.

"He who has pity on the poor lends to the Lord, and He will pay back what he has
given" (Prov. 19:17 NKJV). The Hebrew word for "pity" here means "to in-
cline toward" or to be gracious (Strong's Concordance, No. 2603).

Pity is motivated primarily by the weakness, misery, or degraded condition
of the person being pitied. "We pity a man of weak understanding who
exposes his weakness; we compassionate the man who is reduced to a state of
beggary and want through little or no fault of his own" (Dictionary of English
Synonyms, #1816).

Self-pity, however, is self-indulgently dwelling on one's own sorrows, and
is a form of idolatry and, therefore, a work of the flesh. When we make ourselves the center of creation because things are not going the way we want
them to, then we are idolizing ourselves, and the Bible tells us this means we
are not walking in our Christian rights and privileges (see Gal. 5:19-21).

While our compassion moves us to action on behalf of others, which leads
to our fulfillment and empowerment, self-pity drags us into depression and
brings hopelessness. Self-pity is not kindness to oneself but self-abuse that

causes stress and harm. It reveals a faithlessness by breaking the first commandment in placing oneself higher in importance than God. This obsession with self interferes with God's development of His character in us. When the psalmist couldn't find anyone to pity him, he pitied himself: *"Reproach has broken my heart, and I am full of heaviness; I looked for someone to take pity, but there was none; and for comforters, but I found none"* (Ps. 69:20 NKJV).

GODLY SORROW VERSUS WORLDLY SORROW

I knew a man who had committed adultery, and as a result of his sin, he lost his business, financial security, relationships, the respect he had with others, and even the respect he had for himself. After he repented, he was reunited with his wife. Many of us felt sorry for him and in true Christian style were quick to reassure him of God's love and our love and help; in other words, we pitied him. Later, it became clear that this man's attitude was more of self-pity than genuine godly sorrow. He appeared to have confused the love and support both from God and his fellow man as sanction that he should not have to suffer any consequence to his sin.

Taking responsibility for our actions and facing the painful consequences of our sin are part of God's restoration process. This brokenness is pleasing to God: *"The sacrifices of God are a broken spirit, a broken and a contrite heart—these, O God, You will not despise"* (Ps. 51:17 NKJV).

There is a difference between worldly sorrow and godly sorrow. Second Corinthians 7:10-11 says, *"Godly grief and the pain God is permitted to direct, produce a repentance that leads and contributes to salvation and deliverance from evil, and it never brings regret; but worldly grief...is deadly.... For {you can look back now and} observe what this same godly sorrow has done for you and has produced in you:* (AMP) *What diligence it produced in you, what clearing of yourselves, what indignation, what fear, what vehement desire, what zeal, what vindication! In all things you proved yourselves to be clear in this matter"* (NKJV). True repentance brings godly sorrow that leads to our growth and spiritual maturation. Worldly sorrow is regret at having been found out. We pity ourselves for having to suffer the consequences of our own sinful behavior.

BIBLE CHARACTERS WE CAN LEARN FROM

Jeremiah

"Why do you cry about your affliction [or out of hurt, or because of the natural result of your sins]? *Your sorrow* [pain] *is incurable"* (Jer. 30:15a NKJV).

Jeremiah is asking the people why they are pitying themselves for incurring the penalties of sins they chose to commit. Self-pity says, "Poor thing, suffering for your own sins! It's all right if you sinned. You shouldn't have to suffer for it."

The fact is, *you are responsible for your own actions*. Self-pity involves lying to oneself, because we do deserve to suffer the consequences for our actions. Repentance is the difference between self-pity and godly sorrow. Self-pity is a result of sin, and is incurable without repentance. It has nothing to do with genuine repentance because it's sorry for its suffering and not for its sin. Whereas, godly grief and pain are good for us as they produce the repentance we need for our deliverance.

Moses

When Moses pleaded with God to excuse him from leadership, God rebuked his thinly veiled self-pity as faithlessness (see Exod. 4:10-14). Have you ever told God that He can't use you because of your flaws and imperfections? Moses' self-pity made him unable to trust in the power and faithfulness of God. Don't focus on what you are unable to do and how or why God can't use you. Focus on how great and powerful God is and how all things are possible with Him (see Matt. 19:26).

Jonah

Jonah was so self-absorbed that he not only rebelled against the call of God but also responded selfishly when God reacted to Nineveh's repentance with mercy. God told Jonah those whom he should pity were the 120,000 little children who shared in none of Nineveh's guilt. Remember that self-pity is so self-absorbing, it hinders you from looking beyond yourself to anyone else's problems (see Jonah 3:10–4:11).

David

When David's child became very sick, he did everything he could to save him. But when the child died, David knew there was nothing more that could be done and so he decided to get on with his life (see 2 Sam. 12:15-23).

Our past experiences are the cause of much of our negative attitude and behavior. But while it may be the reason we are the way we are, it is not any reason to stay that way. We must be like David and stop mourning over the past. Don't ruin the time you have left grieving over what has been lost, feeling sorry for yourself and wallowing in self-pity over things you cannot change.

Instead, pledge that you will live each day to the fullest, looking forward to what God has in store for you as you follow Him one step at a time.

Paul and Silas

Paul and Silas overcame their circumstances by praising God. When they found themselves in prison, they did not feel sorry for themselves, but instead, they worshiped the Lord. This hardship was not a result of their own making or due to sin, but was the outcome of following God. Still, they chose to praise God in spite of their terrible circumstances, and God moved on their behalf. As a result, they were supernaturally set free, and were also able to bring the jailer and his family to salvation (see Acts 16:19-35).

When we face trials, we have a choice to either feel sorry for ourselves or to look to the Lord to lead us to victory. Those who pity themselves fail to see God at work in them, while the faithful understand that God always has their best interests at heart.

Self-pity will harden your heart so that you begin to think that life has been unfair to you and that only you matter. Take note: you are special, but not because you were abused, or because you are lonely, or because you went through so much pain when your parents divorced, or because you have a really difficult marriage. You are special because He uniquely, intimately, and wonderfully formed you; He knew you before you were born and called you out then; you are special because He died for you and is forever seated at the right hand of the Father interceding for you; you are special and unique because there is a special call and job that only you can do (see Ps. 139).

WHAT IS THE ULTIMATE CURE?

"Should you not also have had compassion on your fellow servant, just as I had pity on you?" (Matt. 18:33 NKJV). "Pity" here means "to be kind and tender." The simple cure for self-pity is to "pity" someone else: to be kind, tender, and caring for someone else's welfare and interests more than yourself (see Phil. 2:3-8).

The saints who overcome satan and the world are known by the trait that *"they did not love their lives to the death"* (Rev. 12:11b NKJV), or that they are willing to lay down their lives for their friends (see John 15:13). By following Jesus Christ's selfless example, and with the help of the Holy Spirit, we can overcome. Use the hurt you have suffered, including those hurts you have inflicted upon yourself, to comfort and minister to other hurting people.

The ABC's of Emotions

Blessed be the God and Father of our Lord Jesus Christ, the Father of mercies and God of all comfort, who comforts us in all our tribulation, that we may be able to comfort those who are in any trouble, with the comfort with which we ourselves are comforted by God (2 Corinthians 1:3-4 NKJV).

Chapter 17

QUARRELSOME OR QUIET

HOW MANY TIMES A DAY OR WEEK DO WE HAVE the opportunity to quarrel? Yet the Word admonishes us to *"Avoid foolish and ignorant disputes, knowing that they generate strife. And a servant of the Lord must not quarrel but be gentle to all, able to teach, patient"* (2 Tim. 2:23-24 NKJV, emphasis added).

Strife is: quarrelling, bickering, arguing, heated disagreement, angry undercurrent, and even sulking. The English Dictionary defines it as "fighting, heated often violent conflict; bitter dissension; a struggle between rivals; or contention." You should never underestimate the power of strife to destroy relationships in homes, families, and churches. You can feel it in the atmosphere and see it in people's attitudes.

Strife's sole purpose is to destroy, kill, and steal all that is good. More churches, families, and marriages are destroyed because of strife than for any other reason. Jesus said, *"Every kingdom divided against itself is brought to desolation, and a house divided against a house falls"* (Luke 11:17 NKJV). Strife always divides.

Sadly, children pay a high price for strife in families. Many of them daily endure their parents' strife and live with the angry undercurrent. Instead of their home being a safe and peaceful haven, it becomes a war zone, making them angry and rebellious, and damaging them and their future relationships.

STRIFE—NATURAL OR SPIRITUAL?

Let's look at strife for what it really is—a demonic principality and power: *"For we do not wrestle against flesh and blood, but against principalities, against powers, against the rulers of the darkness of this age, against spiritual hosts of wickedness in the heavenly places"* (Eph. 6:12 NKJV).

Joyce Meyer tells the story of a man who refused to settle things with his wife after they had an argument one evening, even though God had prompted him to *"not let the sun go down on your wrath, nor give place to the devil"* (Eph. 4:26b-27 NKJV). In the middle of the night, after not being able to sleep much, God spoke to him and told him He was going to show him what he had given place to in his house because of his stubbornness and rebellion.

In the vision, he saw a large, fierce demon spirit wearing heavy armor—quite unlike the spiritual armor of Ephesians 6:13-17. The demon spirit wore the helmet of pride and the breastplate of unrighteousness; he carried a sword of bitterness and shield of hatred; from His belt hung a hammer of judgment; he wore a cloak of deception; and his feet were shod with boots of anger. He entered, speaking forth lies.[1]

This demon is able to invite in all other trouble-causing demons. Have you ever noticed how you end up having a tremendous fight with someone but forget what started the disagreement in the first place? If you can keep strife and contention out of your life, then you will also be able to keep *"confusion, unrest, disharmony, rebellion and all sorts of evil"* out (James 3:16b).

Are you aware that the devil schemes against you? (See Eph. 6:11). Especially when we are busy and hurried to the point that we become easily annoyed, irritated, and frustrated, we then become easy targets for the devil to bring down and do his will (see 2 Tim. 2:26).

In order to combat him, we must not be ignorant of our weaknesses. Know the process your enemy uses against you and put safety mechanisms in place to resist him. *"Be sober, be vigilant; because your adversary the devil walks about like a roaring lion, seeking whom he may devour"* (1 Pet. 5:8 NKJV).

Jesus said to His disciples: *"Watch and pray, lest you enter into temptation. The spirit indeed is willing, but the flesh is weak"* (Matt. 26:41 NKJV). We must not passively stand by and allow the devil to ensnare us. Take responsibility. The minute you start to blame someone else, you are placing your life in someone else's hands. *"Stop allowing yourselves to be agitated and disturbed; and do not permit yourselves to be fearful and intimidated and cowardly and unsettled"* (John 14:27b).

We have been equipped with an ability and an empowering to walk in divine peace (see Acts 1:8).

THE FOOLISH FLESH

The flesh likes to give its own opinion; it wants to be heard; it likes to be right and wants to have the last say. Another word for *strife* is *contention*, and the definition of contention is to be in a contest. People will fight to be right. Even if they don't feel right about themselves, they still can't stand to be wrong. It's exhausting to live with someone like this. The Bible calls one who sows strife a "perverse person" (see Prov. 16:28).

Some people struggle to get along with themselves and God, never mind anyone else (see Heb. 12:14a). Because they are unhappy with themselves, they are often critical of others and find fault with everything and everyone around them. The Bible says you will love others only as you love yourself (see Matt. 22:39). Although God desires to bless them, they are unable to receive the blessing because strife, confusion, and destruction from the enemy are taking its place.

Pride and self-seeking are the main roots of strife (see Prov. 13:10). And the instrument the devil uses to get the job done is our mouths. An uncontrolled mouth can light and spread strife like a wildfire. While it is easy to find fault with others, the Bible does not give us permission to examine others; we are to examine only ourselves (see 2 Cor. 13:5). Most times God wants us to keep our opinion to ourselves.

"The way of a fool is right in his own eyes, but he who heeds counsel is wise" (Prov. 12:15 NKJV). It takes humility to acknowledge that you might not know it all or be right all the time. Humility, selflessness, and a sanctified mouth stop strife. Perhaps you need to remind yourself from time to time: "I could be right, but I also could be wrong." *"But the wisdom from above is first of all pure (undefiled); then it is peace-loving...(gentle). {It is **willing to} yield to reason**"* (James 3:17a, emphasis added). In any case, your sense of security does not rest on the fact that you are right or wrong. To not be concerned about what everyone thinks of you reveals a maturity and freedom.

At the onset of any trouble and strife, we must resist the flesh. It is much easier to deal with something when it is a minor irritation than a full-blown, heated argument. *"Therefore submit to God. Resist the devil and he will flee from you"* (James 4:7 NKJV).

WHY SHOULD I PURSUE PEACE?

He who would love life and see good days, let him refrain his tongue from evil, and his lips from speaking deceit. Let him turn away from evil and do good; **Let him seek peace and pursue it** (1 Peter 3:10-11 NKJV, emphasis added).

I give mercy because I need it myself.

I can extend mercy and put up with others' faults and weaknesses because I need mercy and grace for my weaknesses and offenses. Maturity and love covers others' sins and extends mercy to its offenders.

I do not want to grieve the Holy Spirit.

The verse, *"Do not grieve the Holy Spirit"* (Eph. 4:30), is sandwiched in between two verses that tell us to put away all corrupt, evil speaking (see Eph. 4:29-32). These types of words do not only hurt and damage ourselves and others, but we grieve the most precious Person in our lives, the Holy Spirit, in the process.

The love walk makes me a spiritual person.

The person who does not quarrel but makes every effort to live in peace with themselves, God, and others is the spiritual man or woman (see 1 Cor. 3:3).

It gives me the power I need.

Often we think a little bit of strife or bickering is harmless and insignificant. Or perhaps we think a big fuss is being made about nothing, but we must come to realize that any amount of disharmony stops God from working. *"Again I say to you that if two of you agree on earth concerning anything that they ask, it will be done for them by My Father in heaven"* (Matt. 18:19 NKJV). God never meant for us to argue all week and live in strife with everyone and then expect major breakthrough when we pray this prayer. We are to live at peace with others and with God, and then this powerful prayer becomes effective.

I will be able to hear God.

When there is unity and peace, we will be able to hear God speak. The peace of God is our umpire telling our hearts which way is right and which is wrong (see Col. 3:15). He will be able to give you direction and work on your behalf only when your mind is clear and undisturbed. He told the Israelites, *"The Lord will fight for you, and you shall hold your peace"* (Exod. 14:14 NKJV). However, you will not be able to hear from God when you are in turmoil and upset, which is the time when you need to hear Him the most.

Seeking peace honors God.

We honor God when we choose to pursue peace, no matter how hard it is and no matter what the cost. He will bless you and honor you for your sacrifice. *"Abram said to Lot, 'Please let there be no strife between you and me, and between my herdsmen and your herdsmen; for we are brethren. Is not the whole land before you? Please separate from me. If you take the left, then I will go to the right; or, if you go to the right, then I will go to the left'"* (Gen. 13:8-9 NKJV). Abram, choosing to avoid strife, gave Lot the first choice. He was determined to pursue peace at any cost and any sacrifice. With that heart attitude, God blessed him far more than Lot (see Gen. 13:14-18).

Some people live with others who are constantly disagreeable, argumentative, and want to always be right. There are two people that quarrelsome people don't get along with—people just like them and people not like them! Keep pursuing peace, however; don't wait for them to adapt to you; resist the devil every time he wants to pull you into strife. God will bless and honor you for that. No two people are really compatible; it takes adjusting and compromising on both sides; it takes swallowing your pride and apologizing even when you think you are right. This is the commitment and decision you make because you have chosen to pursue peace.

LEARNING TO BE QUIET AND FORGIVE

God has given us *two ears and one mouth*, and I believe He expects us to listen twice as much as we talk. Proverbs calls us a fool when we answer a matter before we have heard it properly (see Prov. 18:13). Being quick to listen and slow to speak is a vital skill to acquire in our quest to be less quarrelsome (see James 1:19).

We must follow Jesus' example during a stressful time: *"I **will no longer talk much** with you, for the ruler of this world is coming, and he has nothing in Me"* (John 14:30 NKJV, emphasis added). During the stressful and hurried times of our lives, when we are more likely to get irritated and react in anger, we must learn to be quiet. If things don't turn out the way you wanted them to, realize that this kind of stress is part of life and always will be; learn to let go quickly.

Accusing others, using the words "always" and "never" will be perceived as being quarrelsome and provides no solution. On the other hand, reacting with a "soft" answer will disperse the anger and diffuse the situation rather than aggravating it (see Prov. 15:1).

Don't contend with a fool—someone who is not really interested in understanding but gives their opinion and feels they must always be right. They will only serve to frustrate and anger you.

Finally, remember to forgive. Forgiveness is the surrendering of your right to hurt someone back when they hurt you. *"It is* [a man's] *glory to overlook a transgression or an offense"* (Prov. 19:11b). In other words, even though you notice, you choose to forgive. When we choose to be quiet instead of being quarrelsome, we have chosen a difficult thing, but one with great rewards. Matthew Henry says that "It is a kindness to ourselves, and contributes to the repose of our own minds, to extenuate and excuse the injuries and affronts that we receive, instead of aggravating them and making the worst of them, as we are apt to do." (See Proverbs 12:16b, Matthew Henry's Commentary.)

ENDNOTE

1. Joyce Meyer, *Life Without Strife* (Lake Mary, FL: Creation House, 1995), 10-12.

Chapter 18

REJECTED OR RESTORED

TO UNDERSTAND REJECTION, LET'S FIRST CONSIDER WHAT Jesus endured: *"He was despised and rejected and forsaken by men...and we did not appreciate His worth or have any esteem for Him"* (Isa. 53:3). This chapter is about our struggle when men do not applaud us, but despise, reject, and forsake us—not appreciating our worth or esteeming us. It is in times like these we begin to discover how unpleasant, painful, and soul-destroying rejection can be.

"I hate the double-minded, but I love Your law. You are my hiding place and my shield; I hope in Your word" (Ps. 119:113-114 NKJV). The double-minded are those who were once loyal and trusted as friends but now have become our enemies because of the hurt and pain they have caused us—an experience of betrayal. But we are in good company because Jesus was betrayed by one of His closest allies and disciples, Judas. God can give direction out of rejection, just as He did through Judas' ministry; consequently, Christ was brought to the Cross and fulfilled His destiny (see Matt. 26:14-25 NKJV).

PAIN IS A GOOD INDICATOR THAT GOD HAS A PLAN FOR YOU

Although we should not be controlled by our feelings, we must have access to them. We need to allow ourselves to feel the pleasures and pains of life. Emotional pain is to the spirit what physical pain is to the body. When pain fills our heart, we know we have been wounded in an area in our soulish realm where we need healing and restoration. While we should not let feelings control us, neither can we ignore these signals.

Jesus said, *"Have you never read in the Scriptures: 'The stone which the builders rejected has become the chief cornerstone. This was the Lord's doing, and it is marvellous in our eyes'?"* (Matt. 21:42 NKJV). Jesus concluded that rejection from men is part of God's plan, and it is good.

Joseph, the son of Jacob, who was also betrayed, realized, as Jesus did, that God was working out his rejection for his good: *"But as for you, you meant evil against me; but God meant it for good..."* (Gen. 50:20 NKJV). Recognizing the hand of God in a difficult situation releases you from bitterness. How many times have you realized evil things were necessary in your life so you could receive the consequent blessing and wisdom God wanted to bless you with?

In any case, it is not easy to see the most painful circumstances as being "marvellous" and "for good." Faith is needed not only to overcome problems but to endure them as well. If God is choosing to stand passively by and watch someone reject you, you still must trust He is working it out for your good: *"It is good for me that I have been afflicted, that I may learn Your statutes"* (Ps. 119:71 NKJV).

You are too important to the purpose of God to be destroyed by a situation that is meant to give you character and direction. Although evil does not originate from the heart of God, He will use the thing the devil meant to destroy you with, to perfect what He wants in your future: *"For I know the thoughts that I think toward you, says the Lord, thoughts of peace and not of evil, to give you a future and a hope"* (Jer. 29:11 NKJV).

DIVINE PURPOSE

It is important to understand our destiny as it relates to our relationships. God is too wise to have His plans aborted by the petty acts of men. We have to rely on God's divine plan and protection as we become involved with people. Their access to our future is limited by the shield of divine purpose God Himself has placed on our lives. We obtain freedom when we realize God limits the extent of damage people can do to us. There is always a chance of getting hurt in a relationship because any time you make an investment, there is the possibility of a loss. But there is a difference between being hurt by rejection, and being devastated or destroyed. You may get knocked down, but you should not get knocked out.

Normally, if there is a crash, there is an injury. Although the injury may be serious, we do not have to die in the crashes and collisions of life if we have a seat belt in place. This seat belt will prevent you from more serious injury as it holds you in place. The inner assurance tells you *God is in control* and what

He has determined no one can disallow. If He said He was going to bless you, then disregard anything else and believe a God who cannot lie.

God protects those who belong to Him. He watches over you night and day (see Ps. 121:4). Yet God doesn't intend for every relationship to flourish in your life. There are some cliques, circles, and groups in which He doesn't want you to be included: *"He who has the key of David, He who opens and no one shuts, and shuts and no one opens"* (Rev. 3:7b NKJV). The art to surviving painful moments is responding to God with a "yes" when the doors are open, and a "yes" when the doors are closed.

If God allows the relationship to continue, and some negative, painful betrayals come from it, He is ultimately working it for your good. Sometimes such betrayal or rejection ushers you into a greater consecration and a level with God you would not have reached on your own. He is a loving parent, and the unique thing about God's parenting is He uses a negative to bring about a positive. If no good can come out of a relationship, then God will not allow it. This knowledge sets us free to be transparent.

BETRAYAL CAN BE A FRIEND

If we look at how God views friends, then we see they are ultimately the ones who will help us become all God wants us to be in Him. With God in the picture, we also see that there are people around us who never intend any good for us but bring about blessing in our lives anyway. These types of people we can categorize in the "Judas section." We must widen our definition of friendship to include the betrayer when their betrayal ushers us into the next step of God's plan for our lives.

Consider this account of Jesus' betrayal: *"Immediately [Judas] went up to Jesus and said, 'Greetings, Rabbi!' and kissed Him. But Jesus said to him, 'Friend, why have you come?'"* (Matt. 26:49-50 NKJV, emphasis added).

Every child of God not only has, but also needs a "Judas" to carry out certain aspects of God's divine plan in his life. Judas was, in this sense, a better friend than Peter. We all love friends like Peter who stand ready to protect us with their sword and cut off our enemy's ear. Peter's love, though, was almost a deterrent to the purpose of God. Jesus could have fulfilled His purpose without a Peter but not without a Judas, whose role is crucial to us as he makes us lean on God like never before. We can thank God for those family and friends who are kind to us, but those relationships that are filled with deceit, malice and strife, weakness and failures are often the catalyst for greatness in our life.

Look back over your life and understand it was the persecutions, struggles, and traumas that strengthened you and made you persevere.

The blessings such rejections bring to our lives include:

Dependence on God

God's program for us as we mature in Him is to strip us of our strong human tendency to be dependant on other people, teaching us more self-reliance and total God-reliance. God orchestrates your rejections to keep you from making idols out of other people. God is a jealous God, and He is the only One we should place on a pedestal.

A Well Guarded Heart

Learning the skill of not being moved by others' opinions will be of great gain to you. The apostle Paul said, *"I have learned in whatever state I am, to be content"* (Phil. 4:11b NKJV). You must become tenacious against the rejections of men. How frustrating it must be to want to be used by God but not being able to stand being rejected by men. If you are constantly hungry for man's approval as a people pleaser, then you will not be able to minister to the Lord effectively.

Character

God is more interested in our character than He is in our comfort. *"Count it all joy when you fall into various trials, knowing that the testing of our faith produces patience. But let patience have its perfect work, that you may be perfect and complete, lacking nothing"* (James 1:2-4 NKJV).

A Better Minister

Unfortunately, many people become bitter and not better. Bitterness is a sign the healing process is not over and therefore not ready to be shared. But when we have gone through the full cycle, the experiences in our lives will produce no pain, only peace. If we want to see God's power come from the pain of an experience, we must allow the process of healing to take us far beyond bitterness into freedom.

Faith and Prayer

Faith is the absolute trust and confidence in His goodness, wisdom, and power. Faith is not reserved merely for those things we have or can get, but for those times when there is no other way. Nothing fuels prayer like a need. Your crisis is a privilege because God has given you an opportunity to experience a deeper realm of His miracle-working power. If you are going through a test and you have no way out, it is just a test and there will be a reward. Many times the greater the conflict, the greater the conquest and reward.

FORGIVENESS

"A man who has friends must himself be friendly, but there is a friend who sticks closer than a brother" (Prov. 18:24 NKJV). Too often we have thrown away good people who did a bad thing. We usually forget all the good a friend has done and dwell only on the one bad thing they did to damage us. It is like throwing away an entire car just because one part needs replacing or repair. We must do as Jesus taught us—forgive our debtors because He first forgave us (see Matt. 6:12 NKJV). We all need the gift of acceptance.

"Therefore we also, since we are surrounded by so great a cloud of witnesses, let us lay aside every weight, and the sin which so easily ensnares us, and let us run with endurance the race that is set before us" (Heb. 12:1 NKJV). There is an important race we have to run, but unforgiveness is a great weight that will easily ensnare us and slow us down. Let us forgive everyone who has rejected, hurt, and disappointed us. You may have to forgive someone who has never had the courtesy of saying, "I'm sorry." But do it anyway so the devil doesn't have the advantage over you. Considering what God has done for you, you can't afford not to (see 2 Cor. 2:10-11 NKJV).

RESTORED BY THE FATHER HEART OF GOD

If you are still feeling battered and bruised from the rejections you have endured, then run to the Father, the God of all comfort (see 2 Cor. 1:3 NKJV). It is He alone whom we must trust to see the worst in us, yet still think the best of us. It is the unfailing love of a Father who will watch you go off in immaturity, ignorance, and arrogance; then watch you fail and stumble into sin; but then throw you a party the moment you return to Him (see Luke 15:13-24 NKJV). No matter how foolish we have been, He embraces us with no condemnation or reproach (see James 1:5 NKJV).

It is human nature to try to hide from God the minute we stumble and fall (as if this were possible?—see Gen. 3:8). Do not run *from* God, but instead run *to* Him. Who else knows you like God does? Do not be fearful of Him; He will not reject you (see Ps. 139).

Once we have accepted His Son, Jesus, He wraps us up in His own identity so that we can approach the Father *in Him* when we are in need. Through Him we are able to enjoy a relationship with our heavenly Father and feel comfortable enough to sit in His lap. You are accepted and loved by Him and you can find healing for your scars and bruised heart when you seek shelter in His presence.

> *He who dwells in the secret place of the Most High shall abide under the shadow of the Almighty. I will say of the Lord, 'He is my refuge and my fortress; **My God, in Him I will trust**'* (Psalm 91:1-2 NKJV, emphasis added).

Chapter 19

SUFFERING SHAME

Therefore if any person is {ingrafted} in Christ (the Messiah) he is a ***new*** *creation (a new creature altogether); the old {previous moral and spiritual condition} has passed away. Behold, the fresh and new has come!* (2 Corinthians 5:17, emphasis added).

THE WORD "NEW" REFERS TO SOMETHING THAT IS consecrated, dedicated, or set apart for a different use. When we give our lives to the Lord, He consecrates us for something new and dedicates us for the purpose He originally intended for us.

However, even though we instantly receive a brand-new spirit man, our minds may not yet be renewed. We can retain our "stinking thinking," and the negative strongholds can still remain. My husband often teases me saying, "You can take Marion out of Redhouse," (the village where I grew up) "but you can't take Redhouse out of Marion!" No matter how far or how fast we try to run from our past, we often take it with us because "we don't have it,"—"it has us." The good news is that we can be totally transformed by the renewing of our minds with the Word of God (see Rom. 12:1-2).

In this chapter, we want to study the emotion of shame, how it can remain a stronghold in our life, and how we can renew our thinking with the Word of God concerning this emotion. The New Oxford Dictionary of English defines *shame* as "a painful feeling of humiliation or distress caused by the consciousness of wrong or foolish behavior; or the loss of respect or esteem; dishonour."

God originally intended for shame to be of benefit to us. When we sin, shame motivates us to repent and receive forgiveness. The wise and humble person takes responsibility for his sinful behavior. He feels bad, repents, and receives forgiveness, which then releases and washes the shame from his life. He can then put it behind him without any lasting harm. Whereas, when a proud fool refuses to repent or apologize, he will continue to repeat his mistakes instead of learn from them.

In any case, the amount of shame we suffer can become unhealthy and out of balance in our lives causing severe problems such as depression, loneliness, and anger. Compulsive disorders, substance abuse, eating disorders, money addictions, sexual perversions, to mention just a few, are negative results rooted in shame.

The writer of Psalm chapter 44 experienced an intense struggle with shame. He admits: *My dishonor is before me all day long, and shame has covered my face; at the words of the taunter and reviler, by reason of the enemy and revengeful"* (Ps. 44:15-16). Let's take a look at three important principles from this Scripture.

"MY DISHONOUR IS BEFORE ME ALL DAY LONG"

"Dishonor" or shame was ever-present at this time in his life. A shame-based nature will infect and affect every area of your life. You can't escape the shame because you are not just ashamed of what you have done; you are ashamed of who you are.

If a little girl is sexually abused by her father, she may be ashamed of what is happening to her, but as time passes, a transition will start to take place. She will begin to internalize the traumatic situation and ask herself, "What is wrong with me that makes my father hurt me?" She will conclude that she must have done something to deserve it. The child does not have the insight to blame the adult, but rather blames herself. Because she is unable to distinguish between what is happening *to* her from *who* she is, she develops a totally distorted self-image.

This example applies to abuse of any kind. When things go wrong, the victims do not agonize over what was done wrong, but rather what is wrong with them. They also accept blame for further abuse of any kind. They are plagued with feelings of worthlessness and conclude they deserve to be mistreated.

They develop a disposition of perfectionism, trying to win the attention and affection they feel they never had and were denied. Consequently, they set themselves up for failure as they can never achieve the high standards they have set for themselves. Impossible schedules and unrealistic expectations lead to disappointment and self-hatred which confirms, "I am the problem and the mistake." Feeling like you are failing and never achieving, or are disappointed and discouraged with who you are, is sure evidence of being rooted in shame. And behind this evil scheme is *"the accuser of the brethren,"* the devil, who is trying to destroy your peace of mind and ultimately your life (see Rev. 12:10 NKJV).

When have you last completed a self-inventory? What do you think of yourself? What kind of relationship do you have with yourself? What is your attitude toward yourself? Realize that no matter what you do or where you go in life, you will always have to deal with you! And you should like yourself. In fact, God has commanded us to love ourselves. *"You shall love your neighbor as yourself"* (Matt. 19:19b NKJV). He meant this to be as important as loving others. Often, the people who don't get on with others are the ones who generally don't get on with themselves. If you don't like you, then you will have a hard time liking anyone else.

So how do I like myself? First, separate "your do" from "your who." Let me explain it in these terms: If a child fails an exam, it would be ridiculous to say he is a failure because he failed one time at one thing. In the same way, it is neither rational nor correct to say because you failed at something once, you are a failure. You must learn to separate what you do from who you are.

In addition, it does not mean that if I don't do everything right all the time, God doesn't love me or He won't talk to me. We must be able to make mistakes and still like ourselves. You will find out when you start to like yourself, others will naturally like you too.

Look at yourself in the mirror every day and tell yourself: "I like you; you are a great person; and you have a great personality. You are a child of God and full of the Holy Spirit. You have wonderful talents and gifts, and you are a cool person. I like you." If you do it enough times, you will start to believe it and help yourself overcome a shame-based nature.

Stop cursing yourself. You have the power of life and death in your tongue, and you don't want to agree with the devil and his estimation of you. Resist the temptation to allow what happened in the past determine who you are today. Boldly declare: "I am not what happened yesterday; I endured what happened yesterday; I survived what happened yesterday; but I am not what happened yesterday."[1]

Accept your God-given temperament. This means you come to accept who you are and stop trying to change into something unauthentic. God anoints only that which is true. Making the most of who you are will not only allow you to live in peace but also help you to fulfill your destiny. It is not arrogance to like yourself; it is having confidence in how God sees you as special and unique.

"Shame Has Covered My Face"

Adam and Eve's first reaction after they had sinned was to cover up and hide from God. Sin causes us to experience shame, and shame causes us to hide from God. But before sin, man was "naked" with no secret or shameful place in the presence of God (see Gen. 2:25), which has always been God's intention in our relationship with Him. Being naked before God makes us feel exposed and vulnerable until we remember there is not one action or thought that God has not seen and heard (see Ps. 139:1-12).

Being "naked" simply means being open and vulnerable before God. *"And there is no creature hidden from His sight, **but all things are naked and open to the eyes of Him** to whom we must give account"* (Heb. 4:13 NKJV, emphasis added). The Lord looks beyond our façade and sees our deepest needs. He is aware of everything lurking in the shadows of our hearts—our fears, our failures, and our secrets. We, therefore, have nothing to lose by becoming transparent in the presence of the Lord. Our shame brings loss of self-respect and self-esteem and makes us cover up, close down, and hide from God. So, fight your desperate need for flight. Yes, it is humiliating and painful, but He sees it all anyway; don't run from your very Source of help and salvation.

Perhaps you don't feel accepted by God. But know that you *are* "accepted in the Beloved" (see Eph. 1:6 NKJV). Perhaps you feel your relationship with God is based only on merit. But the fact is, all your works are like filthy rags to God and you can't earn one drop of His blood by merit (see Isa. 64:6; Eph. 2:8). Perhaps you are intimidated by His holiness; understand that you are clothed with Christ and can come into the presence of a Holy God with boldness (see Rom. 13:14). Jesus wraps us up in His own identity, and so we approach the Father *in Him* when we are in need.

God understands you, knows what you have been through, and sympathizes with your weaknesses.

> And there is no creature hidden from His sight, but all things are naked and open to the eyes of Him to whom we must give account. Seeing then that we have a great High Priest who has passed through the heavens, Jesus the Son of God, let us hold fast our confession. For we do not have a High Priest who cannot sympathize with our weaknesses, but was in all points

tempted as we are, yet without sin. Let us therefore come boldly to the throne of grace that we may obtain mercy and find grace, to help in time of need (Hebrews 4:13-16 NKJV).

If you continue to hide from Him, you will never be able to enjoy the relationship you are meant to have with your heavenly Father. You will never feel comfortable enough to sit in your Daddy's lap (see Gal. 4:6). However, the truth is, you are accepted by Him, and you can trust Him to heal your bruised heart if you seek shelter in His presence (see Ps. 91:1-2).

"Blessed are the pure in heart, for they shall see God" (Matt. 5:8 NKJV). God continually sends His cleansing grace into the hearts of His children, but He can't sanctify what we hide in secret. Although He sees all, we must present it all to Him so that He can cleanse and heal our lives and bring peace. He says, *"My grace is sufficient for you"* (2 Cor. 12:9 NKJV).

"AT THE WORDS OF THE TAUNTER AND REVILER, BY REASON OF THE ENEMY AND REVENGEFUL"

The devil is the author of my pain and shame. This is not just a natural fight, but a spiritual one (see Eph. 6:12). It is the accuser of the brethren who is behind the torment of our shame. He wants our destruction and downfall. The good news is God has promised that He will deliver us: *"Fear not, for you shall not be ashamed; neither be confounded and depressed, for you shall not be put to shame. For you shall forget the shame of your youth, and you shall not {seriously} remember the reproach of your widowhood any more"* (Isa. 54:4). The victory is yours already; be determined to reject the roots of shame, and love yourself as Christ loves you. Put an end to feeling unloved and unworthy. When you have messed up, determine to run to God, not from Him. God promises us double blessing and honor for the trouble the enemy has caused in our lives.

> *Instead of your {former} shame you shall have a twofold recompense; instead of dishonour and reproach {your people} shall rejoice in their portion. Therefore in their land they shall possess double {what they had forfeited}; everlasting joy shall be theirs* (Isaiah 61:7).

ENDNOTE

1. T.D. Jakes, *Naked and Not Ashamed* (Shippensburg, PA: Treasure House Publishers, 1995), 47 paraphrased.

Chapter 20

TORMENTED OR TRANQUIL

TORMENT IS DEFINED AS "THAT WHICH CAUSES GREAT PAIN or misery to the body or mind." Scriptures define torment as that which involves fear (see 1 John 4:18 NKJV). Job says: *"How long will you torment my soul, and break me in pieces with words?"* (Job 19:2 NKJV). When someone is tormented, his or her soul is broken into pieces; they have no peace of mind; they are fearful, in pain and misery, and their whole sense of security and confidence is undermined. They are also harassed in their sleep (see Isa. 50:11).

Alternatively, *tranquility* is to be "at rest; peaceful; free from fear or disturbance; and calmness." It is not difficult to understand which is the healthier emotion. *"A calm and undisturbed mind and heart are the life and health of the body"* (Prov. 14:30a). Worrying or fretting disturbs the mind and causes us harm (see Ps. 37:8 NKJV). Whereas, God's best is peace of mind, freedom from fear, tranquility, and calmness; not pain, misery, and the constant fear that something evil is going to happen. We must reject this fear, because it's not His will for us. *"For God has not given us a spirit of fear, but of power and of love and of a sound mind"* (2 Tim. 1:7 NKJV).

People are tormented by so many things: their past, their future, the unknown, others' opinions, failure, not succeeding, not being accepted and loved, being alone, difficult circumstances and situations, and their enemies. Again, we emphasize that torment of any kind is not God's will and originates from our enemy, the devil, who comes to steal, kill, and destroy (see John 10:10).

REASON AND FEAR VERSUS TRUST AND LOVE

"Now the mind of the flesh {which is sense and reason without the Holy Spirit} is death.... But the mind of the {Holy} Spirit is life and {soul} peace..." (Rom. 8:6). We always seem to want to understand everything happening to and around us, using our own human sense and reason. But sense and reason cannot explain God, who is Spirit. He works by His Spirit in the spirit realm for us, and His ways and thoughts are imperceptible to the natural. *"'For My thoughts are not your thoughts, nor are your ways My ways,' says the Lord. 'For as the heavens are higher than the earth, so are My ways higher than your ways, and My thoughts than your thoughts'"* (Isa. 55:8-9 NKJV).

Confusion and frustration are signs you are trying to reason why things are the way they are. We must stop trying to reason and rely on ourselves, as opposed to trusting God. Most times our minds cannot be trusted because it filters our thoughts through its insecurities and rejection. Our limited knowledge and insight also assess situations and circumstances incorrectly. Stop spending endless unfruitful hours worrying about things your mind can't work out.

In intimidating situations that involve disagreement and confrontation, God reassures us: *"...do not worry about how or what you should answer, or what you should say. For the Holy Spirit will teach you in that very hour what you ought to say"* (Luke 12:11-12 NKJV). Worry will exhaust and drain you of your emotional strength. He will be with you to help you say just the right thing at the right time. Jesus said: *"But after I have been raised, I will go before you..."* (Mark 14:28 NKJV). Trust understands that wherever it needs to go, Jesus has already been there. Habitual worriers don't know *how* to trust God. They even worry that they don't trust Him. But God will teach us how to trust Him (see Ps. 22:9-11).

T.D. Jakes writes, "Fear will feed your mind with clutter and weigh you down with the responsibility of feeling like you have to look out for yourself, protect yourself and defend yourself. Fear inflates itself so much that it may make you forget that there is something greater than the self and He is looking out for you."[1] Fear is sin; it wants to control everything in your life and is opposed to trusting God. We must learn to confidently say: *"Yea, though I walk through the valley of the shadow of death, I will fear no evil; for You are with me..."* (Ps. 23:4 NKJV); and *"I will say of the Lord, 'He is my refuge and my fortress; my God, **in Him I will trust**'"* (Ps. 91:2 NKJV).

Fear is the opposite of faith; it is the darkroom where all my negatives get developed. Fear is also the opposite of love. If I love God, then I trust Him fully. My love for Him and my trust in Him will cast out the fear that is in My heart: *"There is no fear in love; but perfect love casts out fear, because fear involves torment. But he who fears has not been made perfect in love"* (1 John 4:18 NKJV).

AN UNDISCIPLINED MIND VERSUS A WELL-BALANCED AND CALM MIND

A *sound* mind is calm and well-balanced and is disciplined concerning what it is allowed to think about. A sound mind is not dependant on circumstances or sense and reason (see 2 Tim. 1:7 NKJV). Sense and reason are based on natural, external circumstances and depending on these will only produce death.

It is interesting to note the different versions of Second Timothy 1:7 *"For God has not given us a spirit of fear, but of power and of love and of **a sound mind**"* (NKJV, emphasis added). Other versions replace *"a sound mind"* with *"self-discipline"* (see NIV) and *"self-control"* (see RSV). A sound mind is not dependant on external circumstances. For example, there are two people in church. The first needs an organ transplant in order to live, but he is always in church worshiping God with joy and peace of mind. The other person has minimal problems, none of which are life threatening, but because of fear and worry, he is unable to open his mouth to worship God. It is never what happens *to us* that determines our quality of life, but rather what happens *in us*.

Many times I refuse to allow my mind to dwell on possible personal failures, failings, or potential danger that might befall my family. On the other hand, I know people who are tormented, even in their sleep, about almost anything (see Isa. 50:11). It is likely that 99 percent of all we allow ourselves to be tormented over will never happen. Don't give yourself the terrible "luxury" of worrying about the "what if's?"

If you allow your mind to dwell on the negatives, then you feed the monster of fear and torment. I see children who are fearful about everything and lack self-confidence because their parents are constantly expressing their fears. These parents teach their children about a world that is fearful, dangerous, and intimidating, instead of telling them about a great God who is well able to keep us.

Whatever rules in our minds is what we have given permission to. The condition to "being kept in perfect and constant peace" is: *"whose mind...is stayed on {Him}, because he commits himself to {Him}, leans on {Him}, and hopes confidently in {Him}"* (Isa. 26:3b). Our disciplined and renewed mind is the key to living in peace and tranquility and moving away from living in fear and torment. Keeping your mind "stayed on Him" means you are in control and you have committed to keeping your mind focused on God, leaning and hoping in Him.

You cannot stop thoughts from coming into your mind, but you can stop from dwelling on them. Starve those things that you want to die in your life, and nurture and feed those things you want to thrive. *"Finally, brethren, whatever things are true, whatever things are noble, whatever things are just, whatever things are pure, whatever things are lovely, whatever things are of good report, if there is any virtue and if there is anything praiseworthy—meditate on these things"* (Phil 4:8 NKJV).

Soul Prosperity or Soul Poverty

If you do not see the value and purpose of spending time alone with God, studying, reading, praying, meditating, and actively putting good things into your mind, then obviously you will never do those things, and you will always have an excuse not to do them. But you need to grow on purpose; you need to be calculating and purposeful as to what you do on a daily basis. Whatever your daily agenda or routine is, will have a compounded effect, for good or bad, for success or failure, for soul prosperity or soul poverty.

Most often, others cannot recognize or determine when we are succeeding or failing, but we *are* constantly succeeding or failing every day. And one day, you and others will feel and see the effects, which will not be hidden or denied!

Ask yourself the question that I have had to ask myself—and be brutally honest: Am I leading my life, or is my life leading me? Do I just accept my life and let other people fill it, or am I in charge of my time? Do I have control over what I think about, or does my mind wander at its own leisure? Sow the right seeds and put into practice a personal growth plan today; then tomorrow will take care of itself.

John Maxwell says, "Successful people conquer their feelings and form the habit of doing things unsuccessful people do not like to do. The bookends of success are starting and finishing. Decisions help us to start. Discipline helps us finish."[2] You are living today in the fruit of whatever seeds you sowed yesterday. If you are tormented by anxieties and stress, running on empty, backslidden, or have no peace and joy in your life, you need to realize that it is the compounded effect of sowing bad seeds in your life. You have made too many withdrawals and not enough deposits. Each of us has been given the same amount of time. Manage and prioritize your time effectively. Spend it wisely by investing it into your soul prosperity.

TORMENT VERSUS CONTENTMENT AND TRANQUILITY

A prosperous soul is one that has a prosperous mind (see 3 John 2). A mind that is peaceful, calm, and not disturbed is one that has learned the secret of contentment.

> *Not that I am implying that I was in any personal want, for I have learned how to be content (satisfied to the point where I am not disturbed or disquieted) in whatever state I am. ... I have strength for all things in Christ Who empowers me {I am ready for anything and equal to anything through Him Who infuses inner strength into me; I am self-sufficient in Christ's sufficiency}* (Philippians 4:11,13).

Contentment has nothing to do with external circumstances but it is a sufficiency that comes from being in Christ.

God is in the restoration business, and He knows how to bring you into a place of tranquility—the place of *"green pastures and still waters"* (see Ps. 23:2-3). He will restore your soul from a tormented to a tranquil one, if you let Him: *"Let be and be still, and know (recognize and understand) that I am God"* (Ps. 46:10a). Finding the Lord for our lives, not only in salvation, but also in peace, in reassurance, in direction, in comfort, in counsel, in provision, and answers to prayers is what we all need to do. And we will find Him if we look for Him: *"For I know the thoughts that I think toward you, says the Lord, thoughts of peace and not of evil, to give you a future and a hope. Then you will call upon Me and go and pray to Me, and I will listen to you. And you will seek Me and find Me, when you search for Me with all your heart.* **I will be found by you, says the Lord**" (Jer. 29:11-14a NKJV, emphasis added).

ENDNOTES

1. T.D. Jakes, *Maximizing the Moment* (New York, NY: G.P. Putnam's Sons, 1999), 54.

2. John Maxwell, *Today Matters* (New York, NY: Warner Faith, 2004), 26.

Chapter 21

UNDERSTANDING AND BEING UNDERSTOOD

WISDOM IS VITAL TO A SUCCESSFUL LIFE. *"Wisdom is the principal thing; therefore get wisdom. And in all your getting, get understanding. Exalt her, and she will promote you; she will bring you honour, when you embrace her"* (Prov. 4:7-8 NKJV).

UNDERSTANDING BEING "IN LOVE"

Relational breakdown is epidemic. The divorce rate has multiplied more than six times in the past 40 years—40 percent of first marriages, 60 percent of second marriages, and 75 percent of all third marriages fail. It is obvious that more and more people do not understand what makes a successful, happy, and healthy relationship.

We can conclude that our prospects for finding more happiness in another marriage or another relationship are not likely. Therefore, pursuing love with our current spouse or friends is usually the best option wherever viable. We must learn how to love and communicate that love so that both parties feel emotionally fulfilled in the relationship.

Most of us enter into marriage because we're "in love." While "in love," the couple become emotionally obsessed and spend hours dreaming and thinking about each other. Togetherness is the ultimate euphoria. During this time, we believe that the other person is perfect, and we remain blind to all their flaws; thus the phrase "love is blind." We believe our love will last forever and is "the real thing." We believe we are different from any other couple who has experienced a failed relationship.

Unfortunately, the "in love" experience is more fiction than fact. The average life span of this romantic obsession is two years—sometimes in the case of an affair, a little longer. When the wave of emotion subsides, and the couple returns to the real world, all their differences are highlighted, and they can be left wondering what they have in common and why they even got married in the first place. The problem is faulty information that the "in love" feeling will last forever.

This experience gives us the illusion that we have an intimate relationship based on mutual love and commitment. There is a feeling of belonging, that we can conquer all problems, and that the other person would never do anything to hurt us. This obsession gives us the false sense that our egocentric attitudes have been eradicated, and we are willing to give anything for the benefit of our loved one. The truth is, none of us is that altruistic.

Gary Chapman, in his book *The Five Languages of Love*, quotes psychiatrist M. Scott Peck's conclusions on that "in-love" experience saying that it is not real love at all for three reasons (paraphrased):

- First, falling in love is *not an act of the will* or a conscious choice. On the other hand, we may not be seeking the experience when it overtakes us.

- Second, falling in love is not real love because it is *effortless*.

- Third, the person who is "in love" is not genuinely interested in focusing on personal growth but rather feels they have arrived.[1]

Gary Chapman continues this point (paraphrased): Real love, on the other hand, while emotional in nature, is not obsessional. It unites reason and emotion.

It is a love that:

1. Involves an act of your will;

2. Requires effort and discipline, and

3. Recognizes the need for personal growth.

Finally Chapman says "Our most basic emotional need is not to fall in love but to be genuinely loved by another, to know a love that grows out of reason and choice, not instinct. We all need to be loved by someone who chooses to love us, who sees in us something worth loving."[2]

Successful, healthy relationships are ones that are constantly being worked on by both parties. Excelling in every field of human life requires great effort. You cannot expect to constantly make withdrawals from your relationships and then be surprised when they fail. One time when Michael and I were arguing, he said, "This relationship should just flow." This is as far from the truth as possible. Anything worthwhile in life has to be worked on—especially relationships.

UNDERSTANDING MEN'S FATHERLESSNESS

We live in a fatherless generation, and even those fortunate enough to have a live-in father often complain that he is absent or passive. These men abdicate their roles as their own fathers did before them. Their reluctance to talk about their emotions comes from the lack of any positive male role model. They are taught "strong boys don't cry" and feel emasculated when you try to get them to talk about emotional issues. Women want their men to be strong and competent but who are also able to share themselves openly and intimately.

Going to the pub or bar, or spending endless hours watching television are forms of escapism and unhealthy coping mechanisms. But if all he knows about a father is one who abdicated the roles of husband and father, then it is not surprising that he also goes AWOL (absent without official leave) emotionally, leaving his partner lonely and learning how to live life without him.

Rob Parsons says, "The real killer is often hidden—they have simply stopped talking to each other. Lack of communication doesn't mean not talking about anything. It means not talking about anything that matters. There comes a point in many marriages where one of the partners either cannot or will not discuss issues that are vital to the other."[3]

It is no secret to both genders that men in particular find it harder to communicate matters of the heart, and it would be easy to excuse men. However, a man having an affair or in the early stages of love doesn't seem to have this problem; therefore, we cannot settle for this excuse.

UNDERSTANDING THE MALE AND FEMALE DIFFERENCES

When things are going well, relationships seem to flow, but when a couple has to navigate the bends and corners in life, problems develop because the genders are wired differently. He navigates one way and she another with disastrous effects.

Men feel they must offer solutions to women's problems. He is goal-orientated and mission-driven, so when she presents problems to him, he feels the need to do something. If these problems seem unsolvable, they make him feel inadequate, and his self-worth is threatened. While she has "de-stressed" by talking to him, he has become stressed by listening.

No matter how career-oriented the woman is, her relationships give her self-worth and esteem. A man's job, however, gives the man his self-esteem and worth. If things are not going well at work, he will struggle with his male ego, whereas if things are going badly at work for a woman, she can cope if her primary relationships are stable.

UNDERSTANDING COMMUNICATION

There is a common saying among real estate professionals which goes "location, location, location." They claim that location is a vital part in the formula of success in acquiring property. We can borrow this phrase for this chapter as I believe the formula for successful relationships is largely due to "communication, communication, communication."

Communication is the umbilical cord of any meaningful relationship. If you retreat into silence, then you will lose your voice and kill your relationship. Speak up, even if it means writing a letter or an email to kick off the conversation.

People talk on five different levels of communication:

- *Cliché* represents the weakest and lowest level of communication such as "how are you" or "how is your family."

- *Factual* where we expose and give nothing of ourselves and invite nothing from others except factual information.

- On the *opinion* level we take the risk of sharing ideas and reveal some of our judgements.

- The *emotional gut* level is about sharing who you really are and talk heart issues and plans.

- The final level of *transparency* is absolute openness and honesty. [4]

For a close and intimate relationship to be healthy and happy, it needs to happen on the emotional gut and transparency levels.

When a husband listens to his wife, he is ministering to her need to be heard and showing that he cares.[5] It is difficult to build a relationship or keep love alive without time. Make time to talk and listen, but also do things with and for each other so that your relationship is sure to succeed. Putting words into action is important as actions either confirm or deny those words. Men who find it strange to show their affection and communicate must adapt. Just because something feels strange doesn't mean it's not authentic.

UNDERSTANDING CONFLICT

Communication implies both a sender and a receiver. Perfect communication requires the receiver to receive exactly what was sent; any imperfection of that message is a distortion. This distortion occurs when the person hearing misunderstands what was said and prevents good communication. The sender and the receiver must be on the same wave length for good communication. When couples disagree, it is easy for them to twist the meaning to their advantage. Too much distortion prevents understanding and reconciliation.[6]

When communication stops altogether and the couple are disconnected from each other, the relationship dies. Divorce signifies that the marriage, which has been failing for months, even years, is over. Very few people enjoy conflict, but it is a vital part of our relationships. It is how we deal with our conflict that makes or breaks our relationships.

Some pointers for constructive conflict are:

1. Don't attack the person; instead deal with the issue. Words create emotion within us, and we will remember how we felt long after we have forgotten what the argument was about.

2. Stay focused on the issue at hand, and don't widen the argument to include other issues. Don't drag up everything under the sun when you are arguing just to add fire power to your arguments. They are usually unrelated and add fuel instead of water to a heated argument.

3. Reflect. Repeat what they have just said to you and add a little of what you are interpreting, asking them if it is correct.

4. Don't recall past mistakes and failings. These are completely unconstructive; they don't allow for change and repentance of past sins; and it shows no intelligence in your negotiations.

5. You don't have to always be right. You may need to say, "I think I am right, but I might be wrong."

6. Remember to major on the majors and minor on the minors.

7. Don't make the issue about the whole relationship. The relationship is far more than one or two issues. If you allow one area of disagreement to determine the whole relationship, you will be doomed to a lot of strife and disappointment.

"Every way of a man is right in his own eyes, but the Lord weighs the hearts" (Prov. 21:2 NKJV). How can anyone really feel that he or she has "won" an argument? It can only be that they lack insight to see the growing resentment, anger, and bitterness that they have left behind. Get used to "losing" some arguments because this is not as important as it seems. Back off and start to listen to the other's side, giving your partner space to express how he or she feels. Conflict is resolved much quicker this way.

UNDERSTANDING FORGIVENESS

We don't realize what a good memory we have been blessed with until we try to forget something. We can't erase memories, but we can decide not to nurture them, as an act of our will. We can decide to forgive as an act of faith. Although you may still feel the pain, don't act on it. Act on your decision to forgive by faith, and soon the pain will disappear, and you will be healed.

ENDNOTES

1. M. Scott Peck, *The Road Less Travelled:25th Anniversary Edition, A new Psychology of Love, Traditional Values and Spiritual Growth* (New York, NY: Touchstone Books, 1978), 89-90.

2. Gary Chapman, *The Five Languages of Love* (Chicago, IL: Northfield Publishing, 1992,1995), 35.

3. Rob Parsons, *The Sixty Minute Marriage* (London, UK: Hodder & Stoughton, 1997), 24.

4. Lathicia Klackers, *Divorce Restoration International Manual*, (Port Elizabeth, South Africa, 2004), 16.

5. Dr Ed Cole, *Communication, Sex and Money* (Tulsa, OK: Albury Publishing, 1987), 51.

6. Ibid, 50 paraphrased.

Chapter 22

VAGUE OR VISIONARY

GOD LOVES PURPOSE. HE IS NEVER VAGUE OR INDECISIVE or unsure about anything. All the way through the Bible, we see how detailed, specific, accurate, focused, and purpose-led He is. His instructions in the Old Testament to Noah concerning the ark (see Gen. 6:8-22), to Abraham concerning the covenant (see Gen. 17:5-14), to the Israelites concerning the tabernacle (see Exod. 25–26) are all precise, and every detail has meaning and purpose. When He gave specific instructions to Moses and Moses didn't follow them exactly, God called it sin and banished him from entering the Promised Land (see Num. 20:7-12).

God requires us to be as purposeful, decisive, and focused as He is. He hates the lukewarm, and promises to vomit out of His mouth those who are neither hot nor cold (see Rev. 3:16). Likewise, those who are double-minded are not pleasing to God (see James 1:6-8).

Most people don't lead their own lives; they *accept* their lives. Unfortunately, life happens to them, rather than the other way around. This chapter is to help us become more focused in those areas of our life where we are not focused, and find out exactly what the Word says He expects of us. We must always hold up the Word of God to our lives as if it is a mirror and examine ourselves to see where we fall short. The Bible says, *"Don't live carelessly, unthinkingly. Make sure you understand what the Master wants"* (Eph. 5:17 TM).

The ABC's of Emotions

IT ALL STARTS IN GOD

"Everything, absolutely everything, above and below, visible and invisible, rank after rank after rank of angels—everything got started in Him and finds its purpose in Him" (Col. 1:16 TM). You will never discover life's meaning or the purpose to your life by looking anywhere else but to God. The starting point to discovering your origin, your identity, your significance, and your destiny can only be in God, anything else is *"a dead end"* (see Rom. 8:6 TM).

Two great days in your life are the day you were born and the day you discovered why. The purpose of your life is significantly greater than your own personal fulfillment, wildest dreams, or happiness. It is by His purpose and for His purpose that you were brought into this world: *"For I know the thoughts that I think toward you, says the Lord, thoughts of peace and not of evil, to give you a future and a hope"* (Jer. 29:11 NKJV).

God has a purpose for your life and planned it before you existed, without your input! He was thinking of you long before you ever thought about Him. *"Your eyes saw my substance, being yet unformed. And in Your book they all were written, the days fashioned for me, when as yet there were none of them"* (Ps. 139:16 NKJV). You do not need to worry as He will fulfill His purpose for your life (see Ps. 138:8a). In God's purpose, even your human error and sin were taken into account. We may be products of our past, but not its prisoners. If God took Moses from a murderer to a formidable leader, and Gideon from a coward to a courageous hero, He can also turn *your* life around.

KNOWING YOUR PURPOSE IN GOD

Knowing your purpose gives your life:

1. *Meaning.* Having a meaning and a purpose causes us to endure; but for a meaningless, purposeless life, nothing is bearable. With focus, we can understand many of the tests and trials we need to go through because *"all things work together for good to those who love God"* (Rom. 8:28a NKJV). He takes our misery and our mess and makes it into our ministry. When we have meaning, we learn to make lemonade out of lemons and our stumbling blocks become our stepping-stones.

2. *Simplicity.* Our purpose becomes the standard we use to measure what is essential in our lives and what is not. People often struggle to say "no" when asked to help, but it is because they are not clear on what their purpose is. They try to do too much and arrive at a

place of burnout and conflict. We call them a "human doing" instead of a "human being." Clear, specific purpose can simplify your life. *"A pretentious, showy life is an empty life; a plain and simple life is a full life"* (Prov. 13:7 TM).

3. *Peace.* Many people are driven into many activities by all the wrong motives. It may be guilt, insecurity, or others' approval, but once we establish our exact purpose in Him, we will maintain our peace of mind. *"You will keep him in perfect peace, whose mind is stayed on You, because he trusts in You"* (Isa. 26:3 NKJV).

4. *Focus.* Purpose concentrates your effort and energy on what's important. You become effective by being selective. It is human nature to get distracted by small issues and we tend to major on the minors instead of majoring on the majors. Michael LeBoef said, "Devoting a little of yourself to everything means committing a great deal of yourself to nothing."[1] Henry David Thoreau said something similar but just as powerful: "One is not born into the world to do everything, but to do something."[2]

There is nothing more powerful than a focused life; the men and women who made the most difference in history were the most focused. The apostle Paul who almost single-handedly spread Christianity throughout the Roman Empire said: *"So let's keep focused on that goal, those of us who want everything God has for us. If any of you have something else in mind, something less than total commitment, God will clear your blurred vision—you'll see it yet! Now that we're on the right track, let's stay on it"* (Phil. 3:15-16 TM).

There are many well-meaning, hardworking, dedicated people who are trying to do it all. They confuse their activity with productivity and often become discouraged when they look back over their lives on what they have accomplished. It is like a builder with no specific plans, so he places bricks in all different places, but never actually builds the house of his dreams. We need to labor to build the house God has told us to build. He is the Chief Architect, and we must build only according to His plans and drawings. *"Unless the Lord builds the house, they labor in vain who build it"* (Ps. 127:1a NKJV).

5. *Motivation.* Purpose produces the passion and energy we need to get the job done. Meaningless work, not overwork, makes us

weary and steals our joy. I love what George Bernard Shaw wrote, "This is the true joy of life: the being used up for a purpose recognized by yourself as a mighty one; being a force of nature instead of a feverish, selfish little clot of ailments and grievances, complaining that the world will not devote itself to making you happy."[3]

6. *Eternity*. Harold Kushner says, "I believe that it is not dying that people are afraid of. Something more unsettling and more tragic than dying frightens us. We're afraid of never having lived, of coming to the end of our days with the sense that we were never really alive, that we never figured out what life was for."[4]

Some people spend their lives trying to create a lasting legacy on earth. They want to be remembered when they're gone, but this is a shortsighted goal. We should work toward building an eternal legacy; our purpose on earth is not to be remembered, but to prepare for eternity. We all have to stand before the judgment seat one day and give an account of ourselves to God (see Rom. 14:10-12). At our final exam, there will be two crucial questions: "What did you do with My Son, Jesus?" and "What did you do with what I gave you?" God will hold you accountable for what you did with your life and all the talents, opportunities, people, and resources He gave you. Did you spend them on yourself, or did you use them for the purpose of God in your life? When you live in the light of eternity, your focus changes from "How much pleasure am I getting out of life?" to "How much pleasure is God getting out of my life?" *"The Lord looked down from heaven on all mankind to see if there are any who are wise, who want to please God"* (Ps. 14:2 TLB).

ADDING VALUE

The Roman poet, Seneca, said, "No man can live happily who regards himself alone, who turns everything to his own advantage. You must live for others if you wish to live for yourself."[5] One of the most significant things a person can do while on this earth is help others. In this life, the measure of a person isn't the number of people who serve him or the amount of money he amasses; it's how many people he serves. The greater your giving, the greater your living. When you add value to others, you do not take anything away from yourself.

Ruth Smeltzer said, "You have not lived a perfect day, even though you have earned money, unless you have done something for someone else who will never be able to repay you."[6]

"The world of the generous gets larger and larger; the world of the stingy gets smaller and smaller. The one who blesses others is abundantly blessed; those who help others are helped" (Prov. 11:24-25 TM). Giving to others naturally changes a person's focus, especially if the giving becomes a lifestyle. Generosity can be simply described as changing one's focus from self to others. When you are occupied with giving to others and helping them succeed, it drives away selfishness. Remember a man or woman wrapped up in self makes a very small package. We must constantly fight selfishness and self-centeredness. *"Self-help is no help at all. Self-sacrifice is the way, My way, to finding yourself, your true self"* (Matt. 16:25 TM).

When you look back on all you have done in life, you will get the most satisfaction from the pleasure you brought to other people's lives. When you invest in another person just for the sake of seeing them blossom, with no thought to any benefit you might receive, you will be the kind of generous person others want to be around. *"The merciful, kind, and generous man benefits himself, for his deeds return to bless him"* (Prov. 11:17a).

Sir Wilfred T. Grenfell said, "The service we render to others is really the rent we pay for our room on this earth. It is obvious that man is himself a traveler; that the purpose of this world is not 'to have and to hold' but 'to give and to serve.' There can be no other meaning."[7] Remember, your value is not determined by your valuables. It is a misconception that you will be happier, feel more secure, or more important if you have acquired more things. Possessions are only a temporary relief and provide only temporary happiness. Self-worth and net worth are not the same thing.

YOUR PERSONAL GROWTH PLAN

Stretch yourself out of your comfort zone but not out of your gift zone. There are two general questions you can ask yourself in order to become more focused on what you would like to do or be involved in:

1. What have I achieved in my life? (This will give you clues as to your competence.)

2. What do I care deeply about? (This will give you clues as to your passion.)

If you struggle to answer these questions, then ask someone close to you to help you.

If you don't have a personal growth plan or a strategy to accomplish your goals, then you will come to this same time next year without having achieved anything within that year. If you have never done anything, start with a realistic plan. Setting yourself unachievable goals will only set you up for failure and discouragement. Success doesn't just happen; it has to be strategized, planned, thought through, prioritized, and documented. Success comes from the compounded effect of a day spent focused and purposeful. It's making good decisions and then having the discipline to stick with them.

If your growth plan is only about you—how you are going to grow and change in order to bless yourself and make yourself more successful, then you have to take a second look. Your growth plan must be based on how you can become wiser and better at helping others. Trust God to help you find His unique growth plan and strategy for your life.

ENDNOTES

1. http://www.maximumimpact.com/Newsletters/Leadership/Archives/2000/06_1.txt

2. http://www.collegemotivation.com/quotes.htm

3. http://www.phnet.fi/public/mamaa1/shaw.htm

4. http://www.randomhouse.com/author/results.pperl?authorid=48314

5. http://www.giga-usa.com/gigaweb1/quotes2/qutophappinessx005.htm

6. http://www.livinglifefully.com/helpfulness.html

7. http://www.excelgov.org/index.php?keyword=a4432c93a04d93

Chapter 23

WORRIED AND WEARY

WORRY IS A HABIT THAT WILL KILL YOU—IT IS EVEN MORE deadly than smoking. Doctors will tell you that there are more people sick in the hospital and in mental institutions, and many more dead, because of worry. Worry, even in its mildest form is wearying, and as every other bad habit or addiction, it doesn't just remain at one stage—it gets worse. And so, there is much to be gained from being worry-free: *"A calm and undisturbed mind and heart are the life and health of the body"* (Prov. 14:30a). Although we understand all the benefits of being *"anxious for nothing"* (Phil. 4:6a NKJV), we may wonder if this is possible. But anything God has put in His Word for us to do and obey is possible and achievable.

There are so many different things that people worry about—the list is almost endless. Indeed, nowhere in the Bible are we promised a trouble-free life, but we are promised His *"power to keep...calm in the days of adversity"* and that we can *"endure whatever comes, with a good temper"* (Ps. 94:13a; Col. 3:12b). God also says, *"Call on Me in the day of trouble; I will deliver you, and you shall honor and glorify Me"* (Ps. 50:15). He may not deliver you immediately or when or how you want delivered, but He will do it. And while we wait, we have access to His power to endure it.

At the root of worry lies fear, driving us to control everything that happens in our life. Fear is actually faith in the negative as we are convinced that something will go wrong and hurt us. Fear embedded in our thought processes causes us to continually reason and try to figure everything out, and worry is our carnal human nature driven by fear attempting to remedy the situation. This effort is tormenting and harassing and will drive us to be overhasty and miss what God has for us (see Prov. 19:2). Worry is a mental habit that we may have had for a long time, which makes it even more difficult to break. The longer you worry, the stronger its hold is upon your life.

Trusting God and walking in peace does not come naturally. It is a skill we must learn and a secret that the apostle Paul discovered: *"I have learned how to be content (satisfied to the point where I am not disturbed or disquietened) in whatever state I am"* (Phil. 4:11b).

Begin to enforce what God has already given you. *"God did not give us a spirit of timidity (of cowardice, of craven and cringing and fawning fear), but {He has given us a spirit} of power and of love and of a calm and well-balanced mind..."* (2 Tim. 1:7).

SIX TRUTHS OF LUKE CHAPTER 12

Jesus taught six key truths in Luke chapter 12 for a peaceful, calm, and well-balanced mind (see Luke 12:22-31 NKJV). Let's study each of these truths to gain a worry-free life.

To Worry Is Sin

*"Therefore I say to you, **do not worry about your life**"* (Luke 12:22a NKJV, emphasis added). Worry is sin, and it will hurt you. The first step is to take responsibility. Many times we don't even realize we are worrying or the extent of it. Instead, we excuse it and feel justified: "Well, you don't know what I have to live with," or "If you had as many problems as I do, then you would also worry," or "If I don't worry, then who will?" These justifications, however, will not lead to repentance or the change we need. Whereas, acknowledgment and repentance of sin will immediately put you back in His presence and restore His peace to your life.

As responsible and competent people doing many good works, we are supposed to *"take"* our responsibility and duties, but "cast" our cares (see 1 Pet. 5:7 NKJV). We tend to get these two confused. Worrying about our responsibilities and commitments makes them burdensome, leaving us exhausted. Yet the Scripture says, *"Cast your burden on the Lord {releasing the weight of it} and He will sustain you; He will never allow the {consistently} righteous to be moved (made to slip, fall, or fail)"* (Ps. 55:22).

Worry is being overly concerned with self and the things of your life; consequently, it produces self-centeredness, which is sin. It does not generate concern for others, but turns inward, thinking only of and for itself. We are not anointed to look after ourselves, only those around us. The healthiest people emotionally are those who have given their lives over to helping other people: *"Let no one seek his own, but each one the other's well-being"* (1 Cor. 10:24 NKJV).

To Worry Is to Doubt God's Provision and Care

"Of how much more value are you than the birds?" (Luke 12:24b). Worry insults God because it doubts His ability and willingness to help us. God tells us over and over how valuable we are to Him and how He watches over us carefully and affectionately. Others may let you down, but God says, *"'I will never leave you nor forsake you.' So we may boldly say: 'The Lord is my helper; I will not fear. What can man do to me?'"* (Heb. 13:5b-6 NKJV). The only way to get rid of your old "stinking thinking" is to renew your mind to His Word (see Rom. 12:2 NKJV). Until you do, worry will continue to rule and destroy your life.

To Worry Means You Will Speak Negative Words

Matthew's Gospel says: *"Therefore **do not worry, saying,** 'What shall we eat?' or 'What shall we drink?' or 'What shall we wear?'"* (Matt. 6:31 NKJV, emphasis added). Worry in your heart will always produce negative and destructive words of doubt and unbelief (see Matt. 12:34-35 NKJV). The power of life and death is in your words, and if you continue to confess death and destruction over yourself and those you love, don't be surprised when it comes to pass (see Prov. 18:21 NKJV).

"Out of the same mouth proceed blessing and cursing" (James 3:10a; see also verses 9-12). Don't spend time with God in prayer and then spend the rest of the day in doubt and unbelief. Change your confession to agree with God's answers, blessings, provision, and care for you. One time I really believed God that a certain gift I had ordered for my daughter's 16th birthday would arrive in time. They had told me that it might or might not be delivered in time, so I started to become anxious. However, I had prayed, so when the temptations came to confess negatively over the situation, which it did on several different occasions throughout the week, I resisted. Each time I chose not to abort my faith in God but instructed myself rather to keep trusting Him for the thing I had prayed for. Today, I can testify to His goodness that He did what He had promised.

If we expect God to do what He has promised, then He expects us to do what we have been instructed to do.

To Worry Is Foolishness

"And which of you by worrying can add one cubit to his stature? If you then are not able to do the least, why are you anxious for the rest?" (Luke 12:25-26 NKJV).

Staying awake at night will not improve or change anything about your problems. In addition, 99 percent of all we worry about will never happen. Our instruction is to: *"Trust in the Lord with all your heart, and lean not on your own understanding"* (Prov. 3:5 NKJV).

Worry in your life means that you are a listener and not a doer. But the Word says, *"Be doers...and not merely listeners to it, betraying yourselves {into deception by reasoning contrary to the Truth}"* (James 1:22). Give up worry, and rest in the fact that you don't know it all, but you know Someone who does: *"For My thoughts are not your thoughts, neither are your ways My ways, says the Lord. For as the heavens are higher than the earth, so are My ways higher than your ways and My thoughts than your thoughts"* (Isa. 55:8-9).

To Worry Means You Have Little Faith

People have different levels of faith, and in the Gospels Jesus commended those of great faith and rebuked those of little faith (see Luke 7:9; 12:28b). An excellent definition of *faith* is: *"...the leaning of your entire human personality on Him in absolute trust and confidence in His power, wisdom, and goodness..."* (Col. 1:4). Worrying is an indication of little faith. Where worry is, there is fear, and where there is fear there is no faith. In order to eradicate fear from your heart, you must trust in God's Word.

Worry is unrest; so to enjoy the "rest" of God, we must believe, trust, and rely on and in God. The fruit of trust is rest. *"For we who have believed...do enter that rest"* (Heb. 4:3a). Do not be discouraged; trust and confidence in God is built up over time and during the course of your walk with Him. As you experience more tests and trials, you will gain spiritual strength and experience and become stronger. Do not give up or give in to worry because soon you will become more than the devil can handle (see James 1:2-4).

To Worry Means You're Seeking the Wrong Things

"For all these things the nations of the world seek after, and your Father knows that you need these things. But seek the kingdom of God, and all these things shall be added to you" (Luke 12:30-31 NKJV). Are you perhaps aiming and striving after something other than God? As Christians we do not have to seek things; we should only seek God; then all that we need and want, He will add to us. I do not want anything that God has not "added" to me, for I know it will not bless me. God does not have a problem with blessing us, and in fact, the Bible says that He takes pleasure in our prosperity; but He does have a problem when things have us (see 1 Pet. 3:4). Seeking after God rather than after

things is a much easier and rewarding pursuit, and it is very precious to Him (see Matt. 6:33).

MAKE A DECISION

Thank God for His Word that corrects us. Remember that His correction is not rejection; it is His direction. We do not have to let worry and anxiety rule us, no matter what circumstances we might be facing. Overcoming starts with a decision. Do not be led by your fickle emotions, but make a decision today based on the Word of God.

> *Peace I leave with you; My {own} peace I now give and bequeath to you. Not as the world gives do I give to you. Do not let your hearts be troubled, neither let them be afraid. {Stop allowing yourselves to be agitated and disturbed; and do not permit yourselves to be fearful and intimidated and cowardly and unsettled}* (John 14:27).

Pursue peace in your life. Desiring it is not enough; an eager, determined, and fervent pursuit is required to bring you the results of a changed mind and life.

> *For let him who wants to enjoy life and see good days...keep his tongue free from evil and his lips from guile (treachery, deceit). Let him turn away from wickedness and shun it, and let him do right.* **Let him search for peace (harmony; undisturbedness from fears, agitating passions, and moral conflicts) and seek it eagerly. {Do not merely desire peaceful relations with God, with your fellowmen, and with yourself, but pursue, go after them!}** (1 Peter 3:10-11, emphasis added).

Chapter 24

X-HAUSTED AND ANXIOUS

WHAT IS STRESS?

IN TODAY'S WORLD IT SEEMS ALMOST IMPOSSIBLE TO live without stress. Even though we have more instant pleasure and convenience than ever before, at the same time the human race is more exhausted and anxious than ever before.

Many find it increasingly difficult to simply survive in the world we live in. Job expresses what many people feel: *"The churning inside me never stops; days of suffering confront me"* (Job 30:27 NIV). In desperation, they seek relief for their problems through any remedy they can find. Our culture is inundated with self-help, therapists, time management workshops, massage parlors, and recovery programs. But there is only one program that has the ultimate cure for stress relief and that is God's manual, the Bible: *"Come to Me, all you who labor and are heavy laden, and I will give you rest. Take My yoke upon you and learn from Me, for I am gentle and lowly in heart, and you will find rest for your souls. For My yoke is easy and My burden is light"* (Matt. 11:28-30 NKJV).

The term "stress" was first used as an engineering term, but now it not only relates to physical pressure but also mental and emotional tension. All stress is not bad, however; God created us to withstand a certain amount of pressure and tension. For example, a chair is built to take a certain amount of weight and physical stress when someone sits on it. If the chair's limits are respected and not exceeded, it should last a long time. But if it is overloaded and abused, and bears weights and loads that exceed its capacity, then it will break. Human beings have also been built to take a certain amount of pressure and stress; but the problem occurs when we come under more weight than we are capable or designed to handle. And once the "chair" breaks, it takes time and effort to fix it, and it may not be put back together exactly like it was originally.

T.D. Jakes says, "Overloaded people fail. They fail at things in their lives such as marriage, ministry, parenting and business. Like an airplane, we can only carry a certain amount of weight. If we have too much baggage on board, we will be ineffective and we won't be able to take off and can even crash. Most people end up exceeding the weight limit. Motivated by the desire to please and impress, they take on too much and, in the end, fail to reach the heights of success or else crash because they ignored their limitations. In order to maximize your life, you have to minimize your load."[1]

We can use another example that describes the levels of stress as an elevator. If we imagine that we have a stress elevator, we can say that the second floor is the normal stress and pressure that God has equipped us to handle. The first floor is the level where we are frequently tired, anxious, irritable, and displaying various symptoms of stress. Our ground floor indicates a level that is closer to meltdown, where the chair legs are beginning to buckle; we are constantly anxious, irritable, and exhausted. And finally, the basement level indicates burnout or breakdown. We must put proper safeguards in place to ensure that we never fall to this level.

Stress affects us both mentally and physically. Mental stress is brought on when we constantly try to figure everything out, worrying, fretting, re-living and repeating issues and concerns without any progress. Because your body doesn't know the difference between real and imagined danger, it will release adrenalin, a God-given hormone that is designed to help you for "flight or fight" in dangerous situations. The same flight or fight response happens in your body whether you are going through real physical danger or just imaginary or emotional trauma. For example, you can lie in bed at night with your heart pounding, your mouth dry, and your body perspiring from fear as you imagine the worst possible outcome.

Physical stress occurs when our bodies get tired and try to tell us that they have had enough; it shouts at us, "system overload!" Years of not listening to our bodies, of little rest, bad nutrition, and pushing ourselves to work harder, will undermine our body's strength and cause many physical ailments. Even though God can heal, we first need to repent for years of disobedience to God for abusing our bodies. *Do you not know that your body is the temple of the Holy Spirit who is in you, whom you have from God, and you are not your own? For you* were bought at a price; therefore glorify God in your body and in your spirit, which are God's" (1 Cor. 6:19-20 NKJV).

WHAT CAUSES STRESS?

"Therefore we do not become discouraged (utterly spiritless, exhausted, and **wearied out through fear)"** (2 Cor. 4:16a, emphasis added).

Fear is the source of all stress (see Gen. 3:7-10). It will exhaust you and cause your mind to be constantly harassed and tormented. The devil uses all our cares and anxieties to kill the power of the Word of God in our lives (see Matt. 13:22). Jesus Himself might appear to you and give you words of encouragement, hope, and life; but your worries and anxieties choke these words right out of you, leaving you burned out and powerless.

You can be motivated by fear or faith—but not both at the same time. Fortunately, fear can be overcome by realizing that God loves and cares for you; consequently, you will stop basing your life's decisions on those things you fear.

There are many things we fear. Worldly ambition is rooted in a fear of being overlooked and of being a failure. Many relationships are based on the fear of being alone or experiencing the pain of rejection. Vanity is based on a fear of being unattractive and unloved. Greed is based on a fear of poverty. Even anger and rage are based on the fear that there is no justice, no escape, or no hope. Stress arises when we try to serve both our fears and God, which is impossible: *"Without faith it is impossible to please Him"* (Heb. 11:6a NKJV).

HOW TO OVERCOME STRESS?

Know Yourself and Your Purpose

Knowing our purpose in life is a key element to reducing stress. Meaning and purpose help us to bear almost anything because we understand why we have to go through tests and trials. We know exactly where God is taking us. It becomes the standard we use to evaluate which activities are essential and which aren't. People who don't know their purpose try to do too much, which causes stress, burnout, and conflict. It is impossible to try to do everything people want us to do. We have only enough time to do God's will.

Purpose-driven people lead less complicated lives and have saner schedules. It concentrates your energy on what's important. You become effective by being selective, as it is human nature to get distracted by small issues. Do less and stop trying to do it all. Prune away even good activities and do only that which matters most.

We need to know when we are at full capacity or reaching overload. We will never remove all the stress, but we can get to know how much we can handle and what our limits are. Our uniqueness will enable us all to handle different amounts of stress, and our warning signs will be different. My eye will start twitching to warn me that I am in overload and at other times I might have heartburn, lack of energy, or disruptive sleep.

Many people may realize they have hit the ground floor of their stress elevator. They know they are producing symptoms such as irrational anger, rash decisions, or have low morale which is uncharacteristic, but they still do not know exactly what is wrong or how to correct it. This person then tends to blame everything and everyone around them for their problems, never thinking that the blame lies within them.

Learn to listen to your body, even when it just needs a short break, some time out, some solitude, or a night alone. When we constantly expect our bodies to reload, refuel, and renew themselves quickly and even instantly, then we will have problems. Finally, learn to respect yourself for who you are rather than what you do.

Obey God

Why is it that people do not listen to the tell-tale signs of their own burnout? It is like a driver who drives a car but never pays any attention to the engine. He looks at the seats and the paint work and thinks they are all looking fine so the engine must be fine too. But if he is only interested in where he's going and how fast he's going, he will soon be on the side of the road with everyone passing him by. He will be left with regret that he should have heeded the warning signs. Don't stop your car only when there's smoke coming out of your hood; take your car in for regular check-ups and services so that you don't have a massive expense and inconvenience of a burned-out engine.

"Obey the promptings of the Holy Spirit" (see Rom. 7:6), which usually involves some minor change that will make a major difference. It is not only the major holidays or time away but obedience to the Holy Spirit in your everyday life that will make a significant difference.

Rest

Men and women constantly push, press, and strive forward. This, along with the everyday wear and tear of living, slowly erodes their soul without them even realizing it. And no average night's sleep will alleviate this tiredness, because it is not just a *body* that is tired, but a *soul*. If farmers know that they must allow depleted soil the time to rest so it can be replenished with what it has given, how much more so for our tired souls.

If you want to be productive, effective, and reach your full potential, then you will have to recognize that once in a while you will need a good rest and break. It is quite amazing that competent, capable people who can do so much do not have the common sense to know that they are tired and need to rest.

"Six days you shall do your work, **but the seventh day you shall rest and...be** **refreshed"** (Exod. 23:12, emphasis added). Never esteem the work that you do as greater than the person who does it. We must know that we all need a place to rest for a moment to rethink where we are and refuel for the journey ahead. Facing the future without rest is like trying to drive a car with the fuel gauge on empty. We do not fail for a lack of giftedness or desire but because we are depleted and ill prepared for the journey. *"The Lord is my Shepherd {to feed, guide, and shield me}, I shall not lack.* **He makes me lie down in {fresh, tender}** **green pastures; He leads me beside the still and restful waters. He refreshes** **and restores my life (my self)...** (Ps. 23:1-6, emphasis added).

T.D. Jakes says, "The truly wise, the truly great, know that they must utilize their resources but not deplete them. Well-timed rest restores your energy and maintains your abilities so that you can function to your full capacity. Too much work, too much stress, being pulled in too many directions will erode your soul and undermine all your efforts. Periodic pit stops will keep you running at peak performance."[2]

Spend Time With God

Imagine Jesus saying this to you today: *"You are worried and upset about many things, but only one thing is needed. {Choose} what is better, and it will not be taken away from {you}"* (Luke 10:41b-42 NIV). Choose to sit at His feet and learn from Him. Spending daily time with Him building a relationship will deposit riches into your life that no trial or tribulation can steal from you. Jesus said we would have many trials and tribulations, distresses and frustrations, disappointments and discouragements; but He has equipped us to overcome them all (see John 16:33). But that equipping happens when we are being still long enough to study His Word, pray, and practice His presence (see Ps. 46:10).

So repent...turn around and return {to God}, that your sins may be *erased...that times of refreshing (of recovering from the effects of heat, of reviving with fresh air) may come from the presence of the Lord* (Acts 3:19, emphasis added).

Take instruction from His Word today:

*Have you not known? Have you not heard? The everlasting God, the Lord, the Creator of the ends of the earth, neither faints nor is weary. His understanding is unsearchable. He gives power to the weak, and to those who have no might He increases strength. Even the youths shall faint and be weary, and the young men shall utterly fall, **but those who wait on the Lord shall renew their strength; they shall mount up with wings like eagles, they shall run and not be weary, they shall walk and not faint*** (Isaiah 40:28-31 NKJV, emphasis added).

ENDNOTES

1. T.D. Jakes, *Maximize the Moment* (New York, NY: G.P. Putnam's Sons, 1999), 13.

2. Ibid., 67.

Chapter 25

YIELDING YOUR YESTERDAYS

Brethren, I do not count myself to have apprehended; **but one thing I do,** **forgetting those things which are behind and reaching forward to** **those things which are ahead,** *I press toward the goal for the prize of the upward call of God in Christ Jesus* (Philippians 3:13-14 NKJV, emphasis added).

THE STORY IS TOLD OF AN OLD CULTURE WHERE PEOPLE USED to attach the corpse of a murdered man to the murderer. As the corpse would start to decompose, its rotting flesh would eat into the flesh of the guilty man, and the poison and decay would eventually end up taking the very life of the living man. This is a good picture of what happens to your soul when you don't *yield your yesterdays* to God. When you carry around dead issues and corpses of relationships, you allow them to drain the life from you, destroying you first emotionally, then spiritually and physically.

Whether you get over your personal history or not, is not based on the level or severity of problems you have experienced. There are people who've had it better than you and done worse, and there are people who've had it worse and done better. It is not what happens *to* you that determines your life, but rather what happens *in* you. How you process the past will determine whether you are able to live a fulfilling, purposeful life or one that is constantly plagued by guilt and regret.

A HEALTHY REVIEW

The Bible says, *"For godly grief and the pain God is permitted to direct, produce a repentance that leads and contributes to salvation and deliverance from evil, and it never brings regret; but worldly grief (the hopeless sorrow...) is deadly..."* (2 Cor. 7:10). God has given us the ability to look over our past and evaluate right from wrong. If we did not have this ability, we would never learn the right lessons and subsequently keep making the same mistakes. The pain we experience is able to produce a good harvest. God does not immediately rescue us from our foolishness so that we don't have to suffer. If He did, He would be a bad parent; and we would never learn that there are consequences to our behavior.

Accepting responsibility for our mistakes and placing the blame squarely on our own shoulders for where we were wrong in past relationships, ventures, and situations is part of God's process. This kind of self-examination produces self-insight and the growth we need to mature in life. Our past is meant to mentor us into becoming wise, insightful, and understanding. *"Be clothed with humility, for God resists the proud, but gives grace to the humble"*(1 Pet. 5:5b NKJV).

The easier option of growth is to learn through God's instruction manual or by taking heed to the instruction of those who He has put in authority over us. The more painful or difficult way to gain wisdom is *"...by actual and costly experience"* (Prov. 5:1a)—by learning from our experiences of yesterday and understanding what we did wrong.

We often experience negative reactions concerning the past, such as being fearful and avoiding such examination. We feel we are failures and cannot cope with the feelings of insecurity and inadequacy that this experience unearths in us. So we do not learn from our mistakes and are doomed to repeat them. On the other hand, we may possess a prideful attitude, which prevents us from accepting any responsibility. We never think we are to blame for anything that goes wrong. We feel no guilt or regret and are also doomed to repeat the same mistakes again.

In either case, God does not want us to fall into the same pothole in the road every time around and has given us abilities to ensure this does not happen.

A PRISONER OF THE PAST

Insecurity and self-condemnation cause us to get *stuck* in overwhelming and crippling guilt over past failures, mistakes, and sins. We make a prison for ourselves where we torture and torment ourselves with images of what could have, would have, or should have been! "If only's" keep us imprisoned in the past, draining us of our strength and energy to move on into our future. Instead of our focus being on what we can do, what we can change, or what we can control in our lives, we make ourselves victims of things we can no longer do anything about.

Bitterness and resentment will never change the past, never correct the problem, and never restore your loss or heal your pain; it will only make it worse. Like skeletons in our closet, they arise at the most inconvenient times to harass us. The devil mocks us with them and makes us feel shameful, inadequate, inferior, and guilty. A *"worldly grief (the hopeless sorrow that...is deadly..."* (2 Cor. 7:10).

We are our own wardens, and we have the keys in our hands. Now that your eyes have been opened, walk right out of that cell you have been imprisoning yourself in (see Isa. 61:1).

Following are three warden keys to yielding your yesterdays: Acknowledge, Authority, and Acceptance.

ACKNOWLEDGE

By this we mean an open and honest confession of all that is holding onto you. David tells us how he overcame: *"When I kept silence {before I confessed}, my bones wasted away through my groaning all the day long. For day and night Your hand {of displeasure} was upon me.... I acknowledged my sin to You, and my iniquity I did not hide. I said, I will confess my transgressions to the Lord {**continually unfolding the past till all is told**}— then You {instantly} forgave me the guilt and iniquity of my sin..."* (Ps. 32:3-5 emphasis added).

When quiet confession to the Lord alone has not brought the peace you so desperately seek, then open confession must be considered. This will break the stronghold of the devil. It can be done publicly under the supervision of a pastor at a water baptism, or more privately to a pastor, counselor, or trusted friend. *"Confess to one another therefore your faults (your slips, your false steps, your offenses, your sins) and pray {also} for one another, that you may be healed and restored"* (James 5:16).

It is only our pride we are protecting when we don't want to tell anyone about our past sin or failures. The devil knows the power of sin is always in its secrecy, so if you can overcome your pride and share with someone you trust, you will receive His promise of mercy. *"He who covers his sins will not prosper, but whoever confesses and forsakes them will have mercy"* (Prov. 28:13 NKJV).

AUTHORITY

"Therefore God also has highly exalted Him and given Him the name which is above every name, that at the name of Jesus every knee should bow, of those in heaven, and of those on earth, and of those under the earth" (Phil. 2:9-10 NKJV). God has given you authority in Jesus' name. He never intended for counseling to take the place of the authority of the believer. When the accuser comes to torment and harass you with flashbacks and dreams of the past, start to use your God-given authority. Claim the promises of God as being your own. Do not passively allow the enemy to torment you by exhuming your corpses. Tell him they are dead and buried, and you don't want anything to do with them.

ACCEPTANCE

Accept that you are fallible and imperfect—always have been, always will be. You cannot be conceited to think you should not have failed, messed up, or sinned as: *"all have sinned and fall short of the glory of God"* (Rom. 3:23 NKJV). Accept that we all need a Savior. Statements like: "I should have known better" will just add to your guilt and torment.

Accept that you have not committed the unpardonable sin and you are not more evil than anyone else. Is your sin worse than David's who committed adultery and murder? Yet God forgave him and called him "a man after His own heart" (see 1 Sam. 13:14). Even the great apostle Paul who wrote two thirds of the New Testament was fallible. If you have sinned and fallen short in some areas of your life, let me personally take this opportunity to welcome you to the human race!

Accept that there will be some things we cannot change, we cannot undo, and we cannot repair. Acceptance will allow you to walk away from the past. Leaving behind dead issues does not mean you are quitting; it means you are conserving your strength for things that count, things you can change, things you can control. It is far braver and more beneficial to recognize that you must move ahead and face new challenges. Focus your energy on things you can actually make an impact on, and bury the past so it may rest in peace. It might help you to imagine putting a gravestone with "R. I. P." written on it next to each of the dead issues in your life. Knowing the difference between those things you can and cannot change in your life comes through wisdom that only God gives.

FORGIVENESS

Forgiveness is still the best medicine for a past problem. God hides His face from all our sin and iniquities and remembers them no more (see Ps. 51:9). He removes them as far as the east is from the west (see Ps. 103:12). God's forgiveness is not a memory lapse, a memory blank, nor amnesia; but it can be best described as a "memory release." Through a process, He brings us to the place where the misery has been pulled out of the memory, as a sting out of an insect bite. You no longer blush from shame when you revisit the memory, nor do tears well up in your eyes. God not only heals the emotional trauma but promises to make you forget the shame of your youth (the past) (see Isa. 54:4). Once we've received the release and the healing, the memory will seem like it happened to someone else.

T.D. Jakes says, "Many times we are judge, jury and prosecutor, giving ourselves a life sentence of misery, mourning and regret. What we need to realize that there is only one Judge and He is forgiving."[1] God is not only forgiving, but He is also merciful and will abundantly pardon you (see Isa. 55:7). Jesus did it all for us by *making our account balance absolving us from all guilt before God*" (Rom. 4:25b).

THE PRESENT

A word you hear today will heal your yesterday. Dr. Lloyd John Ogilvie in *God's Best for My Life*, says, "A sure sign that we have an authentic relationship with God is that we believe more in the future than the past. The past can be neither a source of confidence nor condemnation. God graciously divided our life into days and years so that we could let go of yesterdays and anticipate our tomorrows. For past mistakes, He offers forgiveness and an ability to forget. For our tomorrows, He gives us the gift of expectation and excitement."[2]

God is in the restoration business. *"Do good in Your good pleasure to Zion; rebuild the walls of Jerusalem"* (Ps. 51:18). When David realized the extent of his sin, he started to trust God for His restoration. We too have put our destiny and others' destinies at risk, but God will work all things out for our good. We must trust Him to rebuild where we have allowed destruction.

THE FUTURE

It is impossible to inhale new air until you have first exhaled the old. We can't change where we've been, but we can change where we are going. If you let go of the past, your hands will be free to grab hold of all that God has for you in the future. It takes a strong desire for the future to overcome your present fears and past torment.

God is the only one able to redeem time, and He can restore to you all the enemy has stolen. *"So **I will restore to you the years** that the swarming locust has eaten"* (Joel 2:25a NKJV, emphasis added). He has a wonderful future planned out for you, one full of hope and peace (see Jer. 29:11-14).

Allow the waters of your past to pass by you, taking away your pain and misery, never to been seen again.

> *Because you would forget your misery, and remember it as waters that have passed away, and your life would be brighter than noonday. Though you were dark, you would be like the morning. And you would be secure, because there is hope; yes, you would dig around you, and take your rest in safety. You would also lie down, and no one would make you afraid; yes, many would court your favor* (Job 11:16-19 NKJV).

ENDNOTES

1. T.D. Jakes, *Maximize the Moment* (New York, NY: G.P. Putnam's Sons, 1999), 14.

2. Dr. Lloyd John Ogilvie, *God's Best for My Life - Daily Devotional* (Irvine, CA: Harvest Books, 1981).

Chapter 26

ZEALOUS FOR GOD

Therefore be zealous and repent (Revelation 3:19 NKJV).

A CLOSING NOTE IN OUR FINAL CHAPTER COMES FROM the last Book of the Bible with an instruction that we ought to be zealous. Wherever we are on our journey, in our relationship with God, in overcoming our problems, and in claiming our healing and wholeness, we need to be zealous in order to succeed in our pursuit.

Zealous is defined as "filled with or motivated by zeal; fervent," and *zeal* is "enthusiastic devotion to a cause, ideal, or goal and tireless diligence in its furtherance." The cause, ideal, or goal that we are aiming for is that we grow from spiritual babes into mature believers (see 1 Pet. 2:2), but we will never succeed in that which we are not devoted to or obsessed with. Our desire must be accompanied with discipline and diligence in order to become realized in our lives.

The apostle Paul knew that he had to press and push toward the goal and prize that was laid up for him (see Phil. 3:12-14). Likewise, I have seen some people press toward their prize in God, who have grown more spiritually in a few months than others have in years. They made up for lost time, or redeemed the time, in their lives. Because of their zeal for God and the things of God they chose to seek after Him in all they did. *"But be zealous for the fear of the Lord all the day"* (Prov 23:17b NKJV). Zeal will produce a fast-track growth in your life.

You should also be zealous for the advancement of His Kingdom. Allowing God to heal you and set you free from your past is only the beginning of all that He wants to do with you and through you. He will take you out of the wheelchair and make you the nurse and doctor to others who are in the same position you once were. *"But the people who know their God shall prove themselves strong and shall stand firm and do exploits"* (Dan. 11:32b).

You have been called to do great exploits. Making a difference with your life and adding value to others is what will ultimately bring you the greatest peace and happiness. *"Who gave Himself for us, that He might redeem us from every lawless deed and purify for Himself His own special people,* **zealous for good works"** (Titus 2:14 NKJV, emphasis added).

Bibliography

Augsburger, David. *The Freedom of Forgiveness*. Chicago, IL: Moody Publishers, 1988.

Chapman, Gary. *The Five Languages of Love*. Chicago, IL: Northfield Publishing, 1992, 1995.

Cloud, Henry and Townsend, John. *Boundaries*. Grand Rapids, MI: Zondervan Publishing House, 1992.

Cole, Edwin Louis. *Communication, Sex and Money*. Tulsa, OK: Albury Publishing, 1987.

Cole, Edwin Louis. *Facing the Challenge of Crisis and Change*. Tulsa, OK: Albury Publishing, 1987.

Greening, Kindah. *Grief, the Toothache of the Soul*. Queensland, Australia: Healing Hurting Hearts Ministry, 1997.

Henry, Matthew. *Henry's Commentary on the Whole Bible: New Modern Edition*, Electronic Database. Copyright © 1991 by Hendrickson Publishers, Inc.

Jakes, T.D. *Maximize the Moment*. New York, NY: G.P. Putnam's Sons, 1999.

Jakes, T.D. *Naked and Not Ashamed*. Shippensburg, PA: Treasure House Publishers, 1995.

Landorf, Joyce. *Mourning Song*. Old Tappan, NJ: Fleming H. Revell Company, 1974.

Lloyd, John Ogilvie. *God's Best for My Life - Daily Devotional*. Irvine, CA: Harvest Books, 1981.

Klackers, Lathicia. *Divorce Restoration International Manual*. Port Elizabeth, South Africa, 2004.

Maxwell, John C. *Failing Forwards*. Nashville, TN: Nelson Publishers, 2000.

Maxwell, John C. *Today Matters*. New York, NY: Warner Faith, 2004.

McMillen, S.I. *None of These Diseases*. Westwood, NJ: Spire Books, 1963.

Meyer, Joyce. *Life Without Strife*. Lake Mary, FL: Creation House, 1995.

Parsons, Rob. *The Sixty Minute Marriage*. London, UK: Hodder & Stoughton, 1997.

Peck, M. Scott. *The Road Less Travelled:25th Anniversary Edition, A new Psychology of Love, Traditional Values and Spiritual Growth*. New York, NY: Touchstone Books, 1978.

Phillips, Bob. *Controlling Your Emotions Before They Control You*. Eugene, OR: Harvest House Publishers, 1995.

Wright, Norman. *Recovering From the Losses of Life*. Grand Rapids, MI: Baker Book House Company, 1991.

BOOKS TO HELP YOU GROW STRONG IN JESUS

THE BLOOD OF FAVOR

By Glenn Arekion

"Forasmuch as ye know that ye were not redeemed with corruptible things...but with the precious blood of Christ, as of a lamb without blemish and without spot..." (**1 Peter 1:18-19**).

Does the sight of blood scare you? Make you shudder? Cause you to feel faint? A childhood experience left the author feeling this way for years—until he focused on the "precious blood of Christ" that provides eternal life and love.

Glenn Arekion washes white the truth about:

- Sevenfold Blessings.
- Blood Benefits.
- Curses.
- Keys of Protection.
- Redemption, Remission, Reconciliation.

"And, having made peace through the blood of his cross, ..." (**Colossians 1:20**).

Through every tragedy, tough circumstance, and turmoil, you have been given the gift of peace through His blood. Reach out, reach up—let His loving gift drench you.

ISBN: 88-89127-29-5

Order Now from Destiny Image Europe

Telephone: +39 085 4716623 - Fax +39 085 4716622
E-mail: ordini@eurodestinyimage.com

Internet: www.eurodestinyimage.com

Additional copies of this book and
other book titles from
DESTINY IMAGE EUROPE
are available at your local bookstore.

We are adding new titles every month!

To view our complete catalog on-line, visit us at:

www.eurodestinyimage.com

Send a request for a catalog to:

Via Acquacorrente, 6
65123 - Pescara - ITALY
Tel. +39 085 4716623 - Fax +39 085 4716622

* * * * * * * * * * * * * * * * * * * *

Are you an author?

Do you have a "today" God-given message?

CONTACT US

We will be happy to review your
manuscript for a possible publishing:

publisher@eurodestinyimage.com